D1539486

This book is dedicated to my parents, the late Charles Rothman and Alice Rothman, who were happily married for fifty-eight years—they must have done something right; to my sister and brother-in-law, Janet and Jeff Ware—who also must be doing something right; to Elise Dickerson, my surrogate mom, office manager *extraordinaire*, and all-around factotum; to Linda Jewitt and Lindsay Wilkinson for their support and excellent computer skills; to actress Sondra Locke for her friendship and encouragement and for suggesting that I write this book in the first place; to actress Tina Louise (yes, the *real* Ginger) for her kind words about my final manuscript; in fond memory of my late, beloved cocker spaniel puppy, Zorro, for sitting in bed with me as I was attempting to compose this opus; and, finally, to my beautiful Himalayan kitten, Bear, a true reincarnation of Zorro in almost every respect. Meow.

There never was, I fancy, such stuff put on paper before—
or is this the vanity of every author?
—T. E. Lawrence

Contents

Preface:
Memoirs and the Joy of Writing

As I was completing these memoirs, I read the late Anthony Quinn's autobiography, *One Man Tango*. In it, Quinn states that a man does not write his memoirs to remember. He writes his memoirs to forget. Well, with all due respect to Mr. Quinn, God rest his soul, I have done nothing but remember since completing this book.

But I don't regret writing my memoirs. In fact, I have loved to write all of my life, so it was probably inevitable that I would write my memoirs. And I have never been shy about writing to people from all walks of life.

I think back to my second year in law school at Southern Methodist University in Dallas. I was miserable. I just wanted out of SMU and out of Dallas. I wanted to complete law school and practice law in Colorado. But what to do? I didn't even know that you could transfer between law schools.

However, I had learned that the University of Denver College of Law was about to change its name to honor noted journalist/broadcaster Lowell Thomas. Well, Lowell Thomas was still living. So ... you guessed it. I wrote to Mr. Thomas asking him for his assistance. And, amazingly enough, he wrote me back stating that he would do what he could to help me. I don't know if he ever did anything, but I was accepted by DU for my final year of law school.

1

Then there was the great English actor Paul Scofield, the Academy Award winner for his role as Sir Thomas More in *A Man for All Seasons*. I wrote him a fan letter in 1996, and we became pen-pal buddies for a twelve-year period until his death in 2008.

He was a kind, considerate, and indulgent correspondent. We talked mostly about acting. And he had a wealth of information, with fascinating stories about and insights into the acting profession.

At one point, I called him "Sir Paul," and he told me that he had not had the honor. Well, I was incensed on his behalf, and I wrote to the queen of England requesting that he be knighted. I did get a response from one of the queen's secretaries stating that Scofield would be considered for the next Honours List. What I should have realized, and what Paul later told me, was that he had consistently turned down a knighthood for decades, preferring to remain a "Mister" rather than becoming a "Sir."

One of my great regrets was not flying to England to meet him in person—a lost opportunity that saddens me to this day.

And then there is my friend actress, director, and animal rights activist Sondra Locke. A number of years ago, I was watching *The Outlaw Josey Wales*, starring Clint Eastwood and Sondra. I had never seen the movie before and, frankly, was mesmerized by Sondra.

I had followed her career, fitfully, since she played her Oscar-nominated role in *The Heart Is a Lonely Hunter*, which I saw as a youngster. More to the point, as an attorney, I had followed with interest her litigation against Eastwood and Warner Bros. So I wrote her a nice letter.

The letter was less a fan letter and more a simple letter of acknowledgment and appreciation. And, lo and behold, I received a lovely letter back in response, in which she included her e-mail address. We soon became fast e-mail and telephone friends. In fact, it was Sondra who first suggested that I write my memoirs.

Later, my beloved cocker spaniel, Zorro, was diagnosed with cancer. Zorro was the light of my life, and trying to nurse him back to health was the most trying time of my life. And, God bless her, Sondra was either on the telephone or online with me every day for six weeks helping me to find a cure. Ultimately, our efforts did not succeed. But I will always love Sondra for her efforts and support during one of the saddest periods of my life.

Still later that year, I flew to Los Angeles to have dinner with her for my birthday. And, yes, she was just as wonderful in person. And, yes, I tried my best to impersonate a modern-day Cary Grant and sweep her off her feet. And, no, it did not work. But when you have had Clint … you get the picture. However, I am blessed that I can still count Sondra as one of my friends.

As you can tell, I still love to write letters. Unfortunately, the art of writing letters is dead. I just hope that the art of writing memoirs will remain around for a little while longer, as I just love to read interesting memoirs. I hope that you will find these memoirs of interest and that you will even enjoy a few laughs along the way.

Introduction:
The Conundrum

Mary Ann or Ginger
Tonya or Lara
Betty or Veronica

This choice, my friends, is an important fork in the road for all boys on their way to manhood, or for all men on their way back to boyhood.

As a boy, I never recognized the beauty of the actresses that I saw on television in programs such as *Bewitched*, *I Dream of Jeannie*, *Get Smart*, or even *Leave It to Beaver*. ("What a beautiful dress you have on, Mrs. Cleaver.") In fact, I didn't even think of Elizabeth Montgomery, Barbara Eden, Barbara Feldon, or other similar actresses as attractive girls or women or anything other than characters on TV. Now that I look back on it, I can appreciate the charms of those actresses. They were all quite beautiful women—although I really think that one of the key signs of aging is when you start thinking that June Cleaver (Barbara Billingsley) is actually hot! I even watched *Petticoat Junction*, but, again, the charms of those young actresses as well as the true meaning behind the fictional name of Hooterville completely escaped me. I had an awfully lot to learn.

Then there was *Gilligan's Island*, one of my favorite TV

shows when I was a young boy. Give me a break. I was only ten years old.

Now when I see pictures of Dawn Wells as Mary Ann, I think, "My God, she was gorgeous!" But at the time, dear, sweet, and kind Mary Ann made about as much an impression on me as Gilligan or Mrs. Howell. And before you ask, I still do *not* view Mrs. Howell as a babe—you smart aleck!

No, it was Ginger (Tina Louise), the sexy, conniving bad girl who made the greatest impression on me. Even at that young age, I thought she was *hot*. Every time she attempted to seduce Gilligan, I was a goner. Why? I don't know. Maybe I was genetically predisposed to like the bad girl. Maybe I still am.

And then when I was eleven years old, my parents took me to see my first grown-up movie, *Doctor Zhivago*—another crossroads and a movie masterpiece.

For those of you who haven't seen the movie, it revolves around a young poet and doctor, Yuri (Omar Sharif), his beautiful wife, Tonya (Geraldine Chaplin), and his mistress, the perfect-looking—and I *do* mean *perfect-looking*—siren Lara (Julie Christie).

I really didn't understand the movie very well. The Bolsheviks, the Tsar, the Russian Revolution, and so on were way above my head at the time. But what was clear to me was the life choice that Yuri had to make with respect to his love life.

Should he stay with Tonya, be surrounded by a loving and wealthy family, have a beautiful wife who adored him, and live out a peaceful life in Paris? Or should he pursue that gorgeous temptress, Lara, enjoy brief moments of exquisite bliss, and end up acting out the best death scene in movie history—prematurely aged, clutching his chest, and falling to the ground next to a tram on a lonely Moscow street?

For all you movie buffs, the second-best death scene in movie history is, in my humble opinion, that of David McCallum in *The Great Escape*. But I digress.

If you have ever seen *Dr. Zhivago*, you will recall the scene where Lara is about to go to a party with the villainous character played by Rod Steiger. There is a shot in that scene of Lara dressed up in a gorgeous red gown looking into a mirror. At that point in time and in that scene, Christie was, without a doubt, *the* most beautiful woman in the world—a modern-day Helen of Troy. That scene is indelibly etched into my memory.

In any event, the choice between Mary Ann and Ginger or between Tonya and Lara is the choice that we boys or men all face if, indeed, we have the good fortune to face such a choice at all. As for me, I regrettably have chosen the path leading to Ginger and Lara and, ultimately, disappointment, sadness, and regret. Trust me; I will be avoiding Moscow trams for the foreseeable future. I don't want to tempt fate.

For this purpose, forget about all those music boxes playing "Lara's Theme." Every time I hear one, I want Yuri to run right back into Tonya's arms or, alternatively, I want to smash the box into a hundred pieces. Does anyone really buy those things? When I was in Switzerland, I could not pass a store without seeing and/or hearing one. "Somewhere, my love …" Don't get me wrong. I love the movie soundtrack by the great Maurice Jarre. I just can't stand the lyrics to the theme song.

Finally, on an even lighter note, there is the case of Archie Andrews of *Archie Comics* fame. After sixty-five years of indecision, Archie asked Veronica (and not Betty) to marry him. If only he had consulted with me beforehand, I would have told him that he was making a big mistake. Of course, it is difficult to consult with a comic book character.

And so Archie chose bad girl Veronica (the "Ginger" in his life) over sweet and loyal Betty (the "Mary Ann" in his life). What was he thinking? Obviously, he was *not* thinking.

Yes, Veronica is sexy and desirable, even after sixty-five years. But I was an avid reader of *Archie Comics* in my youth, and I can attest to the fact that Veronica has put Archie through the ringer all these years. And I'm just guessing, but I'll bet that she has cheated on him with Reggie, and maybe even Jughead. (By the way, do comic book characters actually *have* sex?)

Meanwhile, Betty, a very pretty girl in her own right, has been Archie's loyal companion throughout the years. Poor Betty. My advice to her (not that she asked) would be to move out of Riverdale and find herself a real man (and not one with a checkerboard on his head—what's that all about?)

Ultimately, as it turns out, news of Archie's pending marriage was premature. He never did marry Veronica and remains a bachelor to this day. He probably got engaged for publicity purposes—just like a real-life celebrity. But in the end, he probably decided that he could sell more comic books by remaining a bachelor rather than becoming a henpecked husband. Good choice, Archie! My faith in comic book characters has been redeemed.

Speaking of choices (and I believe that I was speaking of choices), I have great stories to tell the grandkids about life and love, but one needs to be able to get a date on Saturday night before grandchildren enter into the picture. In any event, please read on and let me know if I have made any of the right choices.

Chapter One
Groucho, the Little Tramp, and Me

Many years ago, Groucho Marx wrote a book called *Memoirs of a Mangy Lover*. I love that title. (It is even better than Fred Allen's *Much Ado About Me* or Oscar Levant's *The Memoirs of an Amnesiac*.) In his book, Groucho described his many romantic adventures. Unfortunately for him, the book was complete fiction and, to Groucho's everlasting chagrin, it was his brother Chico who always "got the girls" (as they romantically described it in those days).

Chico (pronounced "Chicko," as it was originally spelled) got his nickname because he was a "chick chaser." He was not just a chaser. He apparently caught them all. You can see his charisma as he flirts with beautiful, blonde Thelma Todd in the Marx Brothers' movie *Horse Feathers*. There is no denying it. (Poor Thelma was rubbed out by the Mob shortly thereafter; sad, but true.) There is even a rumor that a much older Chico bedded a much younger Marilyn Monroe when Marilyn had a bit part in the last Marx Brothers' movie, *Love Happy*. I wonder if it really happened. If so, what could she have been thinking? Career advancement, no doubt.

Harpo did all right with the women as well. He never caught them in the movies, but he did so quite often in real life. Poor Groucho was apparently the runt of the Marx litter, and he carried that fact like a gigantic chip on his shoulder all of his life.

By the way, I will use the term *girls* often, as I still tend to think in terms of *guys* and *girls* (but not *Guys and Dolls*—definitely not one of my favorite musicals). And so I will use the term *girls* interchangeably with *women*. I just thought you'd like to know that there is nothing sexist about it—at least, I hope not.

In these memoirs (unlike Groucho's memoirs), you will hear the truth, the whole truth, and nothing but the truth. After all, I am an attorney. All right, no snide comments! Also, the names will not be changed, as there are no innocents to protect. Well, maybe some of the names will be changed to protect me—from lawsuits, that is. On the other hand, truth is an absolute defense to any action for libel or slander. That's a little free legal advice for you—very little.

I have been actively dating since 1960. Yes, I was six years old and in the first grade. Actually, I did have a crush on someone named Debbie in kindergarten, but more on that later.

I am not sure that I will be able to provide any profound advice to readers of this book, but by reading of my many relationships and romantic adventures, you might avoid the mistakes that I have made and maybe even copy the one or two things that I have done right over the years. As I am still single and without children at this late date, you will have to determine for yourself whether or not I have done anything right at all.

But then again, I look at Anthony Quinn and Tony Randall, two men who had children in their dotage. Unfortunately, they are no longer around to see their children grow up. And then there is, of course, Charlie Chaplin, my hero for all sorts of reasons, some even admirable.

Chaplin loved much younger women and suffered legally, financially, and otherwise for his interest (fetish?) By the way,

I think that they called such girls "San Quentin quail" back in the day. Cute, huh? Anyway, good old Charlie had a habit of dating and/or marrying teenage girls. And, then in his fifties, Chaplin married gorgeous eighteen-year-old Oona O'Neill (the daughter of playwright Eugene O'Neill, and the Paris Hilton of the 1940s). He fathered his last child with Oona in his early seventies. Go, Little Tramp, go!

Chaplin was a cinematic genius, of course, and he suffered in many ways for his relationships and/or marriages to much younger women. But in the end, he appeared to have a happy family life and to have found the peace that had eluded him earlier in his life. This is my way of saying that there is always hope … or, at least, I hope so.

As an aside, Emily Dickinson wrote in her poem "Hope" that "Hope is the thing with feathers that perches in the soul …" I love that poem and have read it a hundred times. I just wish that I knew what it meant. Oh, well. I will just have to keep on reading it.

Anyway, let's go back to Chaplin for a moment. As is stated, he was enamored with much younger women. I have read a lot about Chaplin, and I believe that he delighted in these girls' innocence and naïveté. He also enjoyed acting as a mentor and introducing them to the finer things in life, such as foreign travel, art, literature, and the performing arts.

For good or ill, I can relate to Chaplin and feel much the same way—not a good thing for a long and fulfilling love life unless you actually *are* Charlie Chaplin. And I am *not* Chaplin, as you may have surmised.

I think that the attraction begins as a physical attraction. For example, I was a big fan of the adorable *American Idol* contestant Siobhan Magnus and was disappointed when she was voted off the show. I expressed this disappointment to my friend Jessica, who knows me well, and she curtly responded, "Just three words—street urchin complex." Well, I have thought about it and think that maybe she was right.

I do know that younger girls do grow up into mature women and, oftentimes, leave their older boyfriends/husbands/mentors behind.

A great example of this phenomenon is displayed in the wonderful movie *Annie Hall*, in which the older Woody Allen character takes the younger Diane Keaton character under his wing only to lose her in the end.

An even better example is the neglected, but equally wonderful, movie *Beautiful Girls*. In that movie, a thirty-something Timothy Hutton carries on a not-so-mild flirtation with a teenage Natalie Portman. And, yes, even I recognized that this relationship was extremely inappropriate. (However, in my humble opinion, Natalie Portman was then, and continues to be, *the* most beautiful girl in the world.) In the end, the Hutton character drops his pursuit of young Natalie for the clearly stated reason that, even though they are compatible at that point in time, she would soon outgrow him.

That movie made a big impression on me. I can't say that it stopped me from dating younger women. But I can say that it has caused me to pursue such women at my own peril and with my eyes wide open.

Finally, while we are on the subject of younger girls and mentoring, I must relate a quick story about dear, sweet, and *young* Alisa, a former girlfriend whom you will meet shortly. Alisa and I were having dinner with another couple, and the conversation turned to The Beatles. I had just purchased a Beatles CD for Alisa, and she just loved their music. So she became quite engaged in the conversation. At one point, I mentioned the name John Lennon, and she asked, "Who?" I was surprised at her question and told her that he was one of The Beatles. And Alisa responded, somewhat defensively, "Well, I don't know their *names!*" Quite amusing.

Chapter Two
The Best Years of Our Lives

As you have probably already figured out, I love old movies.

One of my favorite American movies of all time is William Wyler's postwar drama *The Best Years of Our Lives*, starring Fredric March, Myrna Loy, Dana Andrews, Virginia Mayo (yum), Teresa Wright, Harold Russell, and Cathy O'Donnell. Never seen it? Put it on your Netflix queue immediately.

The movie revolves around three servicemen in the aftermath of World War II returning to their fictional all-American hometown, Boone City.

Sergeant Al (March), an alcoholic banker, returns to his loving wife of twenty years, Milly (Loy). Bombardier Fred (Andrews) returns to his gorgeous party-girl wife, Marie (Mayo—yum, again), but later falls in love with Al's daughter, all-American girl Peggy (Wright). Meanwhile, disabled vet Homer (Russell) returns, with hooks in place of his hands, to his next-door neighbor/fiancée, Wilma (O'Donnell). Did you get all that?

Was there ever really a town like Boone City? Was there ever really a perfect marriage like the one portrayed between Al and Milly? (Maybe not, as Loy herself was married five times.) Could a next-door romance really flourish between Homer and

13

Wilma, especially after Homer's burnt hands were replaced by hooks? And could upper-class Peggy really have found true love with working-class Fred? I would like to think so.

If I were Fred, I would, of course, have tried to salvage my marriage to Marie—what great legs! And that decision would seem to mirror almost all of my decisions concerning love and relationships: misguided and completely wrong. Did I already mention those great legs?

Well, at least I wasn't alone. Mayo was just one of the many beautiful and anonymous 1940s Goldwyn Girls when Samuel Goldwyn plucked her out of obscurity and made her a star, all because of those great stems.

As you can tell, I just love this movie. And as silly as it sounds, I sometimes use it as a barometer in choosing whom I will and will not date. If the girl is left completely unmoved by the movie, I tend to write her off. But if she enjoys the movie at least half as much as I do, then I conclude that she has a warm heart and is, therefore, definitely worth getting to know.

Chapter Three
Memories of Me

As we are still strangers, let me introduce myself. My name is Barry. I was born at Mount Sinai Hospital in Boone City—hmm, I mean Cleveland, Ohio—on July 7, 1954. I share a birthday with Marc Chagall, Gustav Mahler, and Ringo Starr, but I do not share their artistic abilities, as you will soon learn.

Interestingly, I recently learned that Mount Sinai Hospital no longer exists. You know that you are getting old when the hospital where you were born has been demolished.

My paternal grandparents were from Russian stock. In fact, I do not even know if the family name was Rothman. I am quite sure that it was something else, but the personnel at Ellis Island decided on Rothman—just like Vito Andolini became Vito Corleone in *The Godfather: Part II.*

My maternal grandparents, the Wodickas, were originally from Bohemia, now the Czech Republic. In fact, I was able to trace the Wodicka clan back to Prague in the 1700s, where the family name was Kohn. Possibly, my Bohemian roots are to blame for some of my decision making with respect to love.

I was born with a dislocated hip and was attended to by a specialist and innovator in the field of pediatric hip dislocations at the time, a Dr. Barry Friedman ... hence my first name. The name Barry is Gaelic for "spear." Something sexual, I presume. But you can draw your own conclusions on that one. My mom wanted to name me Robin but was afraid that I would be teased as "Robin Red-Breast." Actually, I would have quite preferred the name Robin. It didn't seem to hurt Robin Williams any.

By the way, my mom told me that Dr. Barry Friedman looked like Tyrone Power. Unfortunately, Barry Rothman does *not*.

Just so you know, I have been compared in looks by many people to the actor Kyle MacLachlan, but, truthfully, I don't see it. He is taller, and I am better looking (he says sheepishly). But then again, you don't see me on *Desperate Housewives*. Damn!

I had a rather *Leave It to Beaver*-type of existence, except that my mom did not wear pearls while she cleaned the house, and my dad did not wear a suit and tie at the dinner table. I always thought that the Cleavers were a bit strange in that regard.

My sister, Janet, was, and still is, two years older than me. And we were, and still are, very close. One of my earliest memories is of a severe snowstorm in Cleveland. I was about three years old, and the snow was over my head, but my sister cleared a path in the snow so that I could actually move up and down the street. That was awfully nice of her. Someday I should thank her. Maybe I just did.

When I was nine years old, we moved to Dallas, Texas—a small, sleepy Texas town at the time, if you can believe it. This move was two months before President Kennedy was assassinated, but I had nothing to do with it. I swear! However, I did carpool to elementary school every day with Jack Ruby's nephews, Brian and Fred. It's true. They were both very nice boys. After the assassination, they quietly moved back to Chicago. For, you see, Dallas seemed to hate Ruby even more than it hated Lee Harvey Oswald. Could it have been because Ruby was Jewish? That was what my parents thought at the time.

As I stated, Dallas was a very different city back then. For example, I was a big wrestling fan as a youngster, and two of the most popular wrestlers in the Dallas area at that time were Fritz Von Erich (complete with Nazi regalia) and Killer Karl Kox (with KKK stenciled on his boots). That never would happen in today's Dallas, or anywhere else, thank God. In any event, once the Ruby children moved away, my brush with infamy came to an end. I wonder whatever became of them.

It is interesting to note that my dad almost witnessed the assassination of JFK. It was a Friday afternoon, and my dad went outside his office building on Main Street to wave at the motorcade. He then went back up to his office, where his secretary told him that Kennedy had been shot. At first, he didn't believe her, as he had just seen the president. Alas, it was all too true. Two days later, on a Sunday, my parents drove down to look at Dealey Plaza, the location of the assassination. Suddenly, they heard and saw an ambulance hurriedly passing by. As it turned out, it was taking Oswald's dead body to Parkland Hospital. Historic!

Anyway, my school years were happy ones, for the most part, with no great traumas. I was not the most popular kid in class, but I was pretty popular and had many friends of both sexes throughout my school career. I was a cheerleader finalist in high school, but I did not get enough votes to become a cheerleader—sad, but not disastrous. But that event kind of mirrored my school social life—not the most popular, but certainly not the least popular.

After graduation from high school, I spent one year at the University of Texas in Austin as a sad and lonely freshman. Then, deciding that I needed to get the hell out of Texas, I spent three years at the University of Colorado in Boulder, where I graduated with a bachelor's degree in business finance. Then I went back to Dallas for two years of law school at Southern Methodist University (back to Texas—what was I thinking?) I finished up law school at the University of Denver, where

I received my Juris Doctor (law degree). I had a love-hate relationship with Texas. Can you tell?

Although I am an attorney, I've always had a love for the fine arts—art, music, acting, dance, etc.— and I have tried my hand at most of these pursuits. I took lessons and played, or attempted to play, the piano, clarinet, flute, and guitar. I actually played the clarinet in the school band for six years.

Much later, I did some acting, was a member of the Screen Actors Guild for three years, and had a memorable (?) performance in a *Perry Mason* made-for-television movie, *The Case of the Scandalous Scoundrel*. It lasted all of ten seconds, but I was so proud. After the movie ended, I called my parents and asked them what they thought. They said, "Were you in it? We must have missed you." Barry, be not proud. (A quick note on my "costars": Raymond Burr—very ill and not to be bothered; Barbara Hale—a real sweetheart; David Ogden Stiers—a real ass; and William Katt—a spoiled brat). I also acted in some local television commercials. Finally, I did some print ad model work, where I was a bit more successful, appearing in a number of newspaper advertisements.

I also took ballet, jazz, and swing dance lessons, even appearing in a production of *The Nutcracker*. I remember one of my ballet teachers always screaming at me, "Barry, your *other* left!" Do you remember the hippos performing ballet in tutus in the Disney movie *Fantasia*? Similarities abound. *Merde!* But I had fun and was able to meet a number of ballet dancers, some of whom you will meet in one of the following chapters.

I preferred ballet dancers to attorneys, but ultimately I stuck with the law. I have often been asked why I became an attorney. The answer that always comes to mind is that I did so because I cannot play the flute like Sir James Galway. But don't get me wrong. I do enjoy the practice of law, as I enjoy teaching and helping people. At least that aspect of the practice of law is satisfying to me.

The nicest compliment that I ever received from a client was that, for an attorney, I had a wonderful bedside manner. And I think that assessment is quite accurate.

After almost thirty years of law practice in Denver, I decided to shake things up and move to my favorite city in the United States, San Diego. (Paris remains my favorite city in the world. *Mais oui!*) I lived in San Diego for a little over a year and tried to build a life there. I met and dated many women. I got involved with the community and found myself wrapping presents for the homeless on Christmas Eve. This nice Jewish boy even joined a downtown church, as the congregation consisted of such a nice group of people. But I never felt completely at home in San Diego.

So I moved to Sarasota, Florida, where I have family, to continue my search for a woman, a satisfying career, a woman, etc. You get the idea. Wish me luck.

One more thing. There is a French proverb that goes something like this: "In love, there is always the one who kisses and the one who offers the cheek." I have always been the kisser/suitor. Maybe it is a function of being a male, or maybe not. But that aspect of my character may explain some of the incidents connected to the relationships described in the following chapters. And just in case you are wondering, I am still "always the one who kisses."

Chapter Four
The Child

Kindergarten: My First Brush with the Opposite Sex

I was in kindergarten, and I noticed her right away.

Her name was Debbie, and she had pretty brown hair, a pretty face, and pretty legs, enhanced by black patent leather shoes and white anklets. (Note the emphasis on the word *pretty*.) I not only noticed Debbie, but I also was aware of the fact that I never looked at any of the other girls in the same way that I looked at Debbie. Nor did I look at any of the boys in the same way. (No homoerotic thoughts for this kindergarten boy!)

And, yes, I did kiss her hand in the cloakroom one day, resulting in a scandal in our kindergarten class. (I think that I saw similar behavior in an old Errol Flynn movie on TV.) But it was not sexual. It was only my first inkling that there was a difference between boys and girls and between certain girls—something that I would learn a great deal more about as I got older.

Conclusion: It was too early in the game to draw any major conclusions. But if you ever find yourself in a cloakroom with a girl, make sure that no one catches you kissing her. Otherwise, you will be grounded, as I was. I still think that treatment was unfair.

First and Second Grade: Kathy the Storm Trooper

I always enjoyed the first week of school each new school year for the very specific reason that I got to scout out the new girls in my class. Very exciting, those first few days of school!

As a schoolboy, I would always differentiate the girls in my class between girls that I noticed the first day (gorgeous), girls that I noticed the second day (very attractive), and girls that I noticed the third day (attractive). I didn't always fall for first-day girls, but invariably I would fall for first-, second-, or third-day girls.

My first relationship lasted two years—pretty good for a first-grader. Her name was Kathy. She had short blonde hair, big blue eyes, and a cute button nose. She reminds me now of a very young, much cuter version of Hillary Clinton, if such a thing is possible.

Unfortunately, sometime during our two years together, she informed me that her parents "hated Jews." *Oy vey!* (Or *oy gevalt*, if you prefer). I had never encountered anti-Semitism before. What was that all about?

My parents grew up as American Jews during World War II, and apparently they used to speculate about which gentile (non-Jewish) families among their friends would hide them if Hitler ever came to power in the United States. I am sure that many American Jews were similarly traumatized during the war, especially given the ferocious nature of the German war machine. Either they would have had to start speaking German or would end up as lamp shades, according to Michael Weiner, a.k.a. Michael Savage, of *The Savage Nation*. Even after the war and my birth, my parents would still evaluate their gentile friends on that basis. Strange but true.

I grew up in a mixed ethnic neighborhood with mostly Italian Americans as my neighbors. I learned early on that my next-door neighbors, the Denallos, would probably hide us from the Nazis, but my across-the-street neighbors, the Salvatores, would probably not hide us. In fact, not only would they probably not hide us, but they would also betray us in the event that they knew where we were hiding. Quite heady stuff for a six-year-old.

Given all that information, the relationship with Kathy had to end. She may not have been a storm trooper, but she was certainly no Miep Gies. (Gies was the woman who helped to hide Anne Frank and her family from the Nazis during World War II. She lived until the ripe old age of one hundred years. Good karma!) I can hear the storm trooper boots as I write this.

Poor Kathy. She probably didn't even realize what she was saying. But I can't make that same excuse for her parents, who should have known better.

Conclusion: What conclusions can anyone draw from a first- and second-grade romance? Well, a flip answer would be that one should never date a Nazi. But a more serious and reflective answer would paraphrase John Lennon's song "Revolution"— don't associate yourself with people with minds that hate. I guess that advice is good, no matter how old you are.

Third Grade: Barry the Two-Timer (Wendy and Celia)

Third grade was a successful year for me.

My regular-school girlfriend was Wendy, a dazzling brunette with a great smile and beautiful brown eyes.

My Sunday-school girlfriend was Celia, a girl with two big brown pigtails and two missing front teeth. That look actually passed for beauty in the third grade.

The year was fairly uneventful, but I was happily busy with two girlfriends. It never even occurred to me that I was a two-timer. Didn't everyone have a regular-school girlfriend and a Sunday-school girlfriend? Maybe not.

Truthfully, I do harbor one regret. A year later, after I had moved to Dallas, I returned to Cleveland to visit my old school chums. However, when I saw Wendy approach, I literally ran away from her and never saw her again. Why did I run? Why didn't I stay and talk to her? I don't know. Later, I was ashamed and disappointed in myself. Still am.

Conclusion: It is never too early to learn good lessons. I should have taken myself over my knee and given myself a good spanking. (A neat trick if it could be done—you try it.) I should also have told myself that one girlfriend at a time was enough for anyone. I think that should be the case for a third-grader or anyone else. Two-timing is never a good idea. Unfortunately, I would disregard that advice many times in the future.

Fourth Grade: Another Two-Girl Year and No Lessons Learned (Linda and Kathy)

Who would have guessed that "the future" would begin the next year, in fourth grade?

This time we were all in the same class at regular school—a potentially more combustible situation. The two girls were Linda and Kathy.

Linda was a very sexy (for fourth grade) brunette with a knowing smile, a twinkle in her eyes, and a cute dimpled chin. Linda was quite advanced for her age and wanted to "make out." I didn't even know exactly what that term meant at the time.

She was adorable, and I was scared to death of her. One time she came at me with open arms, wanting to kiss me. I actually fled in terror. No Cary Grant here.

Kathy was a cute brunette chipmunk-cheeked girl with flashing dark eyes who became a real beauty in high school. Had I known, I would have waited for her.

All of us immature fourth-grade boys used to knock Kathy's pencils off her desk so that we could sneak a peek when she bent down to pick them up. ("I see London; I see France …") Shameful. Homer Simpson would have been proud.

To this day, I never learned whether or not they knew about each other. They must have. Maybe they didn't care, or maybe they were "seeing others" as well. I use that term rather loosely. Remember, this is fourth grade we are talking about.

But with the school year ending, there was summertime with the boys and the hope of a new romance in the new school year.

Conclusion: See third grade above—same conclusion, which reminds me of a scene in the Marx Brothers' movie *Duck Soup*. Margaret Dumont to Groucho: "This is a gala day for you." Of course, Groucho replies to Margaret Dumont: "Well, a gal a day is enough for me. I don't think I could handle any more." Well … it was funny when *he* said it.

Fifth Grade: Diane the Two-Timer

Okay, I'll say it before you do. What goes around comes around. Or, what's good for the goose is good for the gander. I might add, especially as it concerns affairs of the heart. This was the year that Barry got his comeuppance. (I think that I learned this word by reading the stories about young Henry Huggins by Beverly Cleary, which I loved.)

Diane was simply the best-looking girl in the fifth grade.

She had beautiful blonde hair, blue eyes, a dazzling smile, and dark eyebrows. (I've always liked the combination of blonde hair and dark eyebrows.) Picture a young Cameron Diaz—just lovely.

I spent almost all of fifth grade thinking that we were in an exclusive relationship—again, if one can actually be in an exclusive relationship in fifth grade. We never saw each other outside of school. In fact, I don't think that we even talked on the phone. But I felt secure in our "relationship." Unfortunately, Diane moved away at the end of that class year. It was only then that I learned that she had had a second boyfriend. You guessed it. He was one of my best friends, Mitch.

I was beside myself. I was a handsome young boy. Mitch was tall, awkward, and hardly attractive. How could this be? Could Diane have been interested in facets of Mitch other than his less-than-ordinary looks? Could there be interesting things about the opposite sex other than good looks? Did I have so much to learn about these things? Could I learn them, or would I be mentally stuck in fifth grade for all time?

Conclusion: I think that I can now finally answer all of the questions in the prior paragraph. And I think that I might actually be able to answer most of them correctly. You try answering them, and see how you do. Then draw your own conclusions. (You didn't think that there would be a pop quiz, did you?)

Sixth Grade: Robin the Goth, a Version of the Young Avril Lavigne

Her name was Robin, and we were the most popular couple in the sixth grade. We were the Tom Cruise/Katie Holmes of Preston Hollow Elementary School—the talk of the sixth grade. I kind of liked that. She looked like a sixth-grade version of the young Avril Lavigne (kind of Goth, very pretty), and I was in love.

You will note that none of the girls, past or present, will seem to have much in common except that I thought they were adorable. Is this a bad portent for the future?

Anyway, this was love. Robin and I always stared at each other in class, passed notes to each other, ate lunch together, and did all the other things that sixth-graders do. I believe that I even once kissed her on the cheek. In fact, I know that I kissed her on the cheek—more than once. Move over, Rhett Butler.

Robin moved away during the middle of the school year, and I found myself without a girlfriend for the first time since first grade. I was crushed. Why? Because Robin moved away, or because I was left without a girlfriend? When you figure that one out, please let me know. I like to think that I matured during this time period, but as subsequent events will show, I may be mistaken in that assumption.

Conclusion: I don't have one. Maybe had Robin stuck around for the entire school year, I would have had something to conclude about. You may conclude then that I was still clueless.

Seventh Grade: Barry Loses His Groove

Oh, my God! Could I have lost my groove (or my "mojo," as Austin Powers might say) so soon? I fell in love with, in consecutive order, Lucille, Mary Ann (no, *not* Gilligan's Mary Ann), Ellen, and Linda. And … nothing.

What could I be doing wrong? As it turns out, I still don't know. I do know that it was a frustrating year. Unfortunately, I would continue to relive the failures of seventh grade from time to time as I got older.

Speaking of Linda, did you ever know a girl in school whom you were in love with for years, and that love remained unrequited? For me, that girl was Linda. I met her in seventh grade and was in love with her from the first time that I saw her, through high school graduation. We were good friends, but I was never able to switch gears from platonic friendship to romance. All the while, I watched her go from one romantic relationship to the next with an endless series of losers. No, I'm not bitter … just honest. Even many years later, at the few high school reunions that I attended, I always kept an eagle eye out for Linda, but I never saw her again.

My reflections on my past failures (a very painful subject) would not be complete without including all women named Rachel (or Rachael), Sara (or Sarah), and Jessica. I have fallen for many women over the years whose names were Rachel, Sara, or Jessica. And I have never ever been successful at establishing a relationship with someone having any of those names. I can't explain it. Something Biblical, I presume.

Yes, it is always the ones that get away that you think about the most. Ask any fishing enthusiast.

Conclusion: I can just hear Dr. Phil telling me in his distinctive Texas drawl that "It is okay to be alone." And I think that he would probably be right. But believing it and living it are two separate and distinct things. Whenever I am alone, I always feel like it would be better to be with someone. And many times when I am with someone, I feel like it would be better to be alone. There you have the definition of a "bachelor."

Afterthought on Dr. Phil: Have you ever thought that you need analysis twenty-four hours a day? Well, sometimes I envision Dr. Phil following me around, all day and every day, vigorously scribbling in his notepad. Maybe I don't need such analysis, but it couldn't hurt. Are you listening, Dr. Phil? I think that I need a lifetime appointment.

Eighth Grade: Cindy the Shiksa and My Bar Mitzvah

Cindy was the first girl that I ever kissed on the lips. Oh, my! Who invented that? I loved it. As George and Ira Gershwin wrote, "How long has this been going on?" (a brilliant song).

Cindy was an adorable blonde with black horn-rimmed glasses, which only made her more adorable in my eyes. She was also the first girl that I dated who wore makeup. That made her very mature and a big turn-on, at least from an eighth-grader's point of view.

I remember my mother driving me to the movie theater to meet Cindy for my "first date." The movie was *Snow White and the Seven Dwarfs*. I didn't care a thing about Snow White or her dwarfs. All I cared about was sitting in the back of the theater and making out with Cindy, to the great annoyance of everyone around us. But she was such a good kisser. Well, I really had nothing to compare it to, so I can only assume that she was a good kisser.

During that summer, I became a bar mitzvah boy. Besides all the presents that I expected to receive, I was looking forward to "becoming a man." Wow! What was going to happen to me? Would I grow a beard? Would I become Charles Atlas? I knew nothing then, and perhaps very little even now, of testosterone.

I made it through the religious ceremony, faking it all the way. I had not studied very well, so throughout much of the ceremony, I was just throwing out guttural sounds that sounded to me very Hebraic. I could just see poor Rabbi Klein rolling his eyes upward. Later, a non-Jewish friend of my dad's came up to me and told me that, although he didn't speak Hebrew, he could tell that I had really mastered it. At least I fooled someone. Okay, okay, back to Cindy.

After the religious part of the ceremony, I was supposed to be on hand for something called a cake-cutting ceremony. As

I recall, that was where each member of the family would cut a piece of cake and do something with it. Who remembers? It was a long time ago.

However, I was nowhere to be found, and a big search began for the bar mitzvah boy. Finally, my best friend, David, bolted into the temple game room (yes, the temple had a game room!) and found me lying on the pool table making out with Cindy. I was a man after all, wasn't I? I ran back just in time to cut the first slice of cake. Cindy joined me soon after.

It was at that time that "The Scandal" erupted. You see, Cindy was a *shiksa*. What is a *shiksa*? Many Jewish mothers would define the term as "a non-Jewish girl, God forbid." Cindy not only was a Christian but also, God forgive her, she wore a prominent cross around her neck. The Jews in the room, who were, as you might imagine, a majority, were outraged. How dare she wear a Christian cross to a Jewish bar mitzvah? I didn't care. Did I mention that she was a good kisser?

Cindy moved out-of-state shortly thereafter. I just hope that she did not leave with a bad impression of the Jewish people. Maybe just the Reform Jews of Dallas.

Conclusion: I have no regrets about dating Cindy, taking her to my bar mitzvah, or making out in the game room. If I had it to do all over again, I would probably do it the same way, at least with respect to Cindy. But I would take my bar mitzvah a bit more seriously. I probably let a lot of people down that day. It's never too late. I read that Kirk Douglas (a devout Jew) had his second bar mitzvah at the age of eighty-three, as many devout Jews do. That will give me an extra decade or three to brush up on my Hebrew.

Heidi the Drum Majorette

Her name was Heidi. She was of German parentage, and she was the sexiest little blonde Aryan girl that you could imagine. She was also a ninth-grader and was the head drum majorette in the Benjamin Franklin Junior High School marching band.

I, on the other hand, was a not-too-geeky (I promise) eighth-grader who played (or attempted to play) the clarinet in the marching band. I had the biggest crush on her since—well, since forever.

We were friends, but even had she been romantically interested in me (which she was not), she was a year older than me, and no self-respecting ninth-grade girl would ever have a boyfriend who was a mere eighth-grader. I was still crazy about her.

It didn't help matters that I had to play the clarinet and march directly behind her. Let's see … on the one hand, I could pay attention to my marching and the music attached to the music stand on my clarinet. On the other hand, I could pay attention to Heidi's adorable backside dressed in her short drum-majorette's skirt. Well, you now know why I never became the Benny Goodman of my generation.

Heidi moved away after that year. I stayed in the band one more year. But the thrill was gone, as Heidi's replacement was utterly forgettable. However, I will never forget Heidi and the exquisite way in which she marched—unforgettable.

Conclusion: As Mick Jagger sang, "You can't always get what you want." I am not sure that he was referring to Heidi the drum majorette, but you never can tell. If he had only seen her. Yikes! The song continues, "But if you try sometime, you just might find / You get what you need." Mick, I had been trying. I promise.

Chapter Five
The Adolescent

Ninth Grade: Joani the Nonvirgin

Even after my heavy-petting experience with Cindy, I was still a complete neophyte when it came to things sexual—that is, until I met Joani.

Joani said that she was no longer a virgin. I kind of knew what that meant, but the implications were completely lost to me. She sure did like to talk about her sexual past, probably just to get a rise out of me, either figuratively or literally, or both. In looking back on it, I think that she was probably just as much a virgin as I was, but I was very gullible—still am.

Joani was from the other side of the tracks. I was from an upper-middle-class background, and she was from the lower classes. But she intrigued me, due in no small part I am sure, to the fact that she was light-years ahead of me, sexually speaking.

She claimed to have something called "skin attacks," which meant that she liked to take my shirt and pants off. Then what? I never figured it out, and if she had been as experienced as she claimed, she would have helped me to figure it out. By the way, these skin attacks did not go both ways. Joani never shed any clothes as I remember, and I think that I *would* remember. But I went along with it. Who wouldn't at that age, even if it was very embarrassing on double dates?

Joani was also the first girl that I encountered whose actions and personality scared me. She was extremely jealous. She called at least four or five times a day and was extremely moody. At the time, all I knew to do was to break up with her as a form of self-preservation. That aspect of her was quite scary, and I would experience it with other girls later on. I had a choice to make—put up with her antics in the hopes of more sexual experiences, or run away and run away fast. I ran. ("Run, Forrest, run!")

Joani left my life as abruptly as she came into it (no pun intended). Even at that young age, I considered it a blessing. I hope that she finally found peace and happiness.

On a lighter note, I was recently reminded of a funny story related to Joani. One day my friend Bruce, Joani, and I were hanging out in my bedroom and were very bored. My sister had on her bookshelf the book *The Joy of Sex*, which was relatively new at the time. To this day, I still don't know how my parents allowed it. In any event, I got the book, Bruce read of the various sexual positions described, and Joani and I acted them out (fully clothed, mind you). The three of us thought that it was hilarious. Well, my mother, who is generally very laid back, charged into my bedroom like a bull moose and told us to knock it off (in so many words). We did not feel that we had done anything wrong, but we did as we were told. To make matters worse, I don't think that I learned anything. Damn.

Conclusion: I don't care whether you are in ninth grade or ninety years old—when you encounter someone with seeming personality disorders, run, don't walk, out of that relationship. This advice does not apply if you are in a committed relationship and your significant other begins exhibiting problems—I am not one to be speaking about that issue. But if it is a new relationship, watch out for warning signs, be aware, and be prepared to leave unless you want to devote your life to trying to help someone who may be beyond your help. Don't try to play Florence Nightingale or Mother Teresa—it's just not worth it.

Bonnie and the Imaginary Camera

Bonnie was simply the sexiest girl that this ninth-grader had ever seen. Her skin, her eyes, her nose, her teeth, her figure, her legs … oh, my! We were in a few classes together and were platonic friends. Nothing more.

Poor Plato—did he ever have any girlfriends? I haven't done my research, but I believe that young boys were his thing. To each his own.

Unfortunately, in our classes together, I just could not stop staring at Bonnie. One day she finally got angry and said, "Take a picture. It will last longer." I didn't know what she meant. She explained it to me. I like to think that it cured me from further staring at her, but I don't think that it did. In fact, I know that it did not.

Whatever happened to Bonnie? Well, I saw her at a high school reunion a number of years ago, and bless her heart, she had turned into Rosemary Clooney or Stevie Nicks—she was as big as a tent. I felt terrible. For her or for me? I'm not sure. But I sure was sorry to see her that way. "The way we were," indeed.

Conclusion: None really. Just a tinge of sadness. We all get older, and some of us age better than others. It's called "life."

Afterthought on high school reunions: As I get older, it seems to me that there is a high school reunion planned every year. I know that it is not really so, but it sure seems like it. I guess that it is a function of age and of time passing more quickly.

Many people hate their ten-year high school reunion, as they feel that most people are there to show off how well they have done over the past ten years. Well, there certainly is some of that. But I really enjoyed mine. It was close enough in time to high school that I enjoyed seeing everyone and still had a lot to talk about with them.

The next (and last!) reunion that I went to was my twenty-fifth reunion. And, frankly, I was bored to death. I just didn't have a whole lot to say to anyone. I kept looking around thinking to myself, "Who *are* all these old people?"

I ended up being cornered by an old classmate whom I remembered as Brent. We were not particularly close in high school, and I didn't have much to say to him. But I couldn't seem to make a graceful exit. Added to that was the fact that Brent had undergone a sex change operation and was now known as Jo Bren. Well, he/she still looked like Brent to me, except that Brent now had longer hair and breasts. And I kept thinking to myself, "I flew to Dallas for *this?*"

I haven't been back to Dallas since then. I guess that is what Facebook and other social websites are for. You can have your very own high school reunion without leaving the comfort of your home. And good luck, Jo Bren, wherever you are.

Tenth Grade: Shari the Friend

My relationship with Shari was probably the healthiest one of my life up until that time, which may not be saying much. She was a nice Jewish girl from down the street whom I had known since elementary school. A very sweet girl.

Somehow, she had blossomed into a striking brunette, and I was smitten. It was such a nice relationship, as we were just very good friends who also were romantically interested in each other. Then somehow, for some reason, the relationship morphed back into a nice friendship. And that was just fine with me.

Later on, I acted as her "beard." Let me explain. Shari's parents were strict Orthodox Jews who did not allow her to date non-Jews. Oh, the intolerance of some people! Anyway, my best friend at the time, Rod, was very interested in Shari, and vice versa. But, oh my God, he was a non-Jew. What to do? Well, I would pick her up, drive her to my house, transfer her to Rod's car, wait for them, transfer her back to my car, and take her home. It was all very altruistic of me.

Rod and Shari dated for some time, but ultimately and much later, Shari married a well-connected, wealthy attorney who, of course, was Jewish. Her parents were thrilled. As I understand it, they still are.

On a side note, Shari's house always smelled like macaroni and cheese. I could never figure that one out. It's funny the things that we remember. Every time that I think of Shari, I think of mac and cheese and vice versa.

Conclusion: A wise old man once told me to marry your best friend. I would presume that he meant that you should also date your best friend. Good advice. She may not be the best-looking girl, the most intelligent, or the best in bed (God forbid), but you will have an equal partner through life, and that ain't half-bad.

Eleventh Grade: Jill the Body Beautiful

As I look back on Jill (which is, in itself, a wonderful experience), I must admit that she had the greatest body of any girl that I have dated, either before or since. And since I am a typically shallow male, I have dated many girls with exquisite figures. In any event, I was madly in love with Jill (or with Jill's body—you decide).

However, my attempts at lovemaking, or at least making out, were completely one-sided. She was one of those girls who would undress and allow you to do anything (within reason) to her body, but she absolutely refused to reciprocate. Did I care? You know the answer.

Jill lived in a scary old house and had a scary old mother. Think of the Addams Family house with a very ugly Morticia Addams ruling the roost. I would brave it and her mother and visit Jill at her home anyway. You can guess why.

Jill also lived very far away, and I did not yet have a car. But with lust in my heart, I completely destroyed my favorite bicycle by riding to her house every day. Just think about it: I wore out my new bike in exchange for frequent encounters with Jill. Well, I guess that it was worth it.

One such visit is still ingrained in my memory. Jill had two boyfriends at the time, me and another whose name escapes me. Let's just call him "the Jerk." No, I'm not a bitter person. Well, maybe just a little. Anyway, one night, both of us came to court her. She placed me in one room and the Jerk in another room. She would come to my room, kiss me, and tell me that she was trying to get rid of the Jerk. Then she would go to the other room, containing the Jerk, and tell him the same thing about me.

We both knew what was going on, but our hormones were raging, and so we both stayed put … did I tell you about that body? Ultimately, she ended up with the Jerk. And, frankly, that was just fine with me.

After high school, I learned that she married the Jerk. No hard feelings. They were probably deserving of each other. I wonder if they are still married. And what has become of that body? Gravity, I suspect.

Conclusion: This is an easy one. Don't ever play the fool for anyone—especially if you know that you are doing so. Forget the girl, the body, and the sex (yes, all of those), and keep your self-respect. It is worth more than all of those other things by at least a hundredfold. Trust me on this one. Also, your bicycle will last a lot longer.

Twelfth Grade: Roslyn the Heartbreaker

Roslyn was a "younger woman." I was a senior in high school, and she was a sophomore. Two years' difference means nothing as one gets older. But in high school, two years seems like a big difference. I've always loved younger women.

I am getting ahead of myself here, but I have always subscribed to a memorable quote often attributed to Tony Curtis (a.k.a. Bernie Schwartz—true): "I could never date anyone old enough to be my wife." Yes, it's a memorable and funny quote, but not one to live your life by, as you shall see in subsequent chapters. Although, as I understand it, it generally worked for Tony—lucky guy.

Roslyn was a dark-haired, dark-eyed Kewpie doll with a great figure. She was cute as a dewdrop, and she knew it. These looks were, of course, post-braces and post-nose job—seeming prerequisites for teenage Jewish girls. She was from one of those families with many daughters, each one more beautiful than the other. How does that happen? It must be something in the water—in this case, in Cleveland's water supply, as she, too, was originally from Cleveland.

Roslyn and I dated my entire senior year. I remember always being proud to be with her, as she was so sweet and beautiful. And I remember just doing those things that high school couples do. I also remember that she was very concerned that we would "go all the way." I calmed her fears and told her that I would not let that happen. And I didn't. I felt very protective of her. But what I remember most of all was our breakup at the end of my senior year—heartache.

On or about my eighteenth birthday, lovely Roslyn broke up with me, and I was devastated. I was completely heartbroken for the first, but regrettably not the last, time in my life. You know the feeling—like a truck has driven across your chest. Horrible! Of course, you fantasize about all the good things about her, even if they weren't true. You don't know how you will ever get over it. You call her on the phone just to hear her voice and hang up. You even peer over her fence to see if she is with anyone else.

Of course, today this kind of behavior might be considered "stalking" by some and can have rather unfortunate consequences. And once as I was peering over her fence one night with my friend David (you met him earlier at my bar mitzvah), I was stopped by a policeman who told me to forget about her and go home. A policeman dispensing advice to the lovelorn. I think that his badge actually said "Officer Dr. Phil." That's something you're not going to see on the next episode of *Cops*.

Anyway, one does finally get over such things. Time heals all wounds or, as Groucho would say, "time wounds all heels." I wish it were so.

One funny story that I later heard about her concerned her engagement to her future husband. Okay, I know that hearsay is not admissible in court, but it is a great story, and I believe it to be true. After her future husband presented an engagement ring to her, her parents had him return the ring and exchange it, as the diamond had not been large enough to satisfy them. Her fiancé dutifully bought her a larger ring. Cute, huh? I would like to think that I would have reacted a bit differently.

Twenty years later, I ran into her again. She had been married for almost twenty years, had two children, and was about to get divorced. Another ring dispute? She had just had her breasts lifted ("not enlarged, just lifted," she emphasized to me), and she was quite proud of them. And, yes, they looked and felt fine. However, it seemed like we didn't have much more to talk about other than her breasts. Obviously, there was no "click" remaining, and we went our separate ways. However, I do wish her and her breasts nothing but the best. And I mean it.

Conclusion: When it's over, it's over. Let it go. I know that it is tough—maybe one of the toughest things that you will ever do—but some things are just not meant to be. If these sound like overused clichés, they are, but you will find that they are all true and can all be applied to life, love, and the pursuit of happiness.

Chapter Six
The College Boy

Freshman Year: Cindy the Bad Kisser

Unlike many of my peers, I did not enjoy being a freshman at the University of Texas. I was still grieving over my breakup with Roslyn. I hated fraternity life. And, generally, the freshman girls were more interested in upperclassmen than mere freshman boys.

So I was thrilled to be fixed up with a nice Jewish girl named Cindy. She was very sweet, and I liked her a lot. The trouble was that she had never learned how to kiss.

Cindy kissed in a closed, mush-mouth fashion, and I was beside myself with frustration. She could have just been inexperienced, or she could have been using it as a ploy to keep me at a distance. And she sensed my frustration, but she was either unable or unwilling to do anything about it. And so it was not fated to last and did not last for more than a couple of months.

Conclusion: Kissing is important! If a girl does not kiss well, you can pretty well be assured that she will not be competent in performing other acts of a sexual nature. On the other hand, if she is a good kisser, she will probably be good at other things as well. This is not a guarantee. But I think that it is a pretty reliable guideline to follow.

Not Losing My Virginity at the Chicken Ranch

As I discuss in the next section, I lost my virginity as a junior at the University of Colorado. I had reached the ripe old age of nineteen, as had my girlfriend, Stacey, when we both made love for the very first time for both of us. We were in love and dated for three years. It was all very romantic, and I wouldn't change a thing about losing my virginity at that age and to that girl.

However, I did have the opportunity to lose my virginity as a freshman. My fellow fraternity members were about to embark on a trip to the Chicken Ranch in La Grange, Texas. It is closed now, but it once was famous as "the best little whorehouse in Texas."

Actually, I wish that I had gone with them—not to partake in the services offered, but just to passively observe the proceedings in that very well-known establishment. But, no, I even refused the opportunity to go and observe.

So what did I do instead? I took a tour of the Lyndon B. Johnson Presidential Library adjacent to the UT campus. In retrospect, I think this was a bad choice on my part. The Chicken Ranch is now just a memory (for some!) The opportunity to check it out is gone forever. The LBJ Library is still there and will be there forever. I could have visited it at any time. Oh, well. We live and learn.

Conclusion: I probably did not miss much in La Grange. But, I still wish that I had gone there—again, just to observe, mind you. I swear!

Sophomore through Senior Year: Stacey the Model

We called her "the model," we being the guys who used to take the bus daily from our dorm to campus at the University of Colorado. We called her the model, as she was tall and statuesque and carried herself in an elegant manner.

Stacey had long brown hair down to her lovely hips, beautiful hazel eyes, a cute turned-up nose, and a glorious smile. Picture Katharine Ross in *The Graduate*. ("Elaine! Elaine!") And each and every one of us was afraid to approach her.

However, one night toward the end of my sophomore year, we ran into each other at a bus stop, and the rest is history, which is to say that we began a romantic relationship. College was out for the summer, though. I was stuck in Dallas, she was in Denver, and the days could not pass quickly enough for either of us. This was true love—at least, I thought so and still do.

Finally, I got back to school for my junior year, and Stacey and I made love for the first time—and I mean the first time for both of us. It was kinda romantic when I look back on it, at least until she started to bleed shortly after we completed our lovemaking.

Thinking myself a man of the world, I applied a cold compress to the affected area, but the bleeding would not stop. Finally we went to the university clinic. I was not allowed in with her, but she told me later that they had to stitch her up. Horror! "They," whoever "they" were, also told her that we had "done it wrong." To this day, I am still confused. How can two people do it wrong? Anyway, we continued doing it and, apparently, started doing it right, as we had a very satisfactory sex life during our three years together.

Specifically, I remember one hot day during summer school.

Stacey was wearing white short-shorts, we were both twenty-one years old, and we made love five times in about an hour and a half (a record I now approach only in my dreams). We were very compatible and good friends. Maybe I was learning a thing or two.

I even took her home to Dallas to meet my parents. She and my mom disliked each other instantly. To this day, I don't know what the problem was, but at the time it posed a problem for me because I wanted my mom and girlfriend to get along. Today I'm not so sure that I would care quite as much.

I asked my mom about this episode in preparation for this book. She said that she and Stacey had driven past our temple, and my mom had pointed it out to Stacey as the place where my sister had recently gotten married. My mom felt that Stacey, as a Catholic, was probably offended for some reason. I just felt like a precursor to Rodney King in thinking, "Can't we all just get along?" Unfortunately, we all just couldn't get along.

Later, we both graduated, and I returned to Dallas for law school, without Stacey. Why? I think in retrospect that it was not a wise move. But she had been the only girl that I had known in the Biblical sense, and I felt, rightly or wrongly, that I needed to meet and sleep with more girls before getting married.

Our, by now, long-distance relationship limped along for almost a year until, inevitably, she found someone else. It served me right, but I was devastated (shades of Roslyn ... remember her?) It took me quite a while to get over her, but I think that I finally made it.

However, for the sake of curiosity, I did recently hire a private detective to track her down. He did—in Oakland, California. He gave her my particulars and told her that I would like to hear from her. I am still waiting. Don't worry. I am not holding my breath.

Finally, the following fact is one that is important for all guys to recognize. Remember this: all girls turn into their mothers, sooner or later. By this, I mean that all girls will start looking, if not acting, like their mothers over time. As I mentioned, Stacey was a Katharine Ross, circa 1967. Unfortunately, her mother was an Eleanor Roosevelt, circa 1945. The last time that I saw Stacey—fully ten years after our relationship ended—I could see Eleanor start to make great inroads into Katharine. Things probably did work out for the best after all, or did they?

It is interesting to note that I became well known as the guy who was dating Stacey. I am sure that my male classmates would look at us and wonder, "What the hell does she see in him?" During my undergraduate years and thereafter, I was known as the lucky guy in the business school who dated the girl with the long brown hair.

Even years later, after I became an attorney, those people who attended the business school with me didn't necessarily remember me, but they did remember that there was someone who was always hanging out with Stacey and, when I told them that it was me, they seemed to put the pieces into place and remember me for the simple fact that I was Stacey's boyfriend. I guess that it is just nice being remembered for any reason, even if it is for something having very little to do with you.

Conclusion: She was my best friend for a very important three years of my life, so, in retrospect and despite her mother/ Eleanor, I think I might have made a mistake in not marrying her. But as another wise old man once told me, the past is the past, and never kick yourself over mistakes that you might have made in the past. (I'm going to have to stop talking to wise old men!)

Law School: Rhonda, My Very Own Laura Bush

Every couple should have a good "first meeting" story. This one is not my best story, but it is a pretty good one.

I was clerking after my first year of law school at a law firm in downtown Dallas. Still licking my wounds from the breakup with Stacey, I was anxious to meet someone new. An associate in the firm had told me about a cute and single court reporter who had been in the office taking a deposition just two weeks before I started working there.

I called her and reminded her that we had met at our law office during the deposition (a lie on my part; utter confusion on hers). I asked her if she would like to get together for dinner. She accepted, and we met that night. Smooth—dishonest, but smooth.

Rhonda was a sweet, homespun type of girl from Pecos, Texas, with a wonderful personality and a great Texas twang to her voice. The folks loved her. In fact, looking back over all the women in my life, I think she probably would have made the best wife and mother.

So what was wrong with me? Well, I was still quite shallow at the time. Her figure was a bit fuller than was my wont. In addition, she was a virgin when we met, and the sex was just so-so. I was never very interested in teaching.

Although we spent two years together, the relationship did not flourish. This was my fault. I should have been more compassionate in and out of bed. She was quite willing. I was just rather removed from it all. Maybe I was still thinking of Stacey. More likely, I was just thinking of myself.

Later, however, after I moved back to Colorado, she introduced me to the joys of phone sex. How seemingly out of character for her and what a turn-on. Here was this sweet, virginal girl from the Bible Belt in Texas telling me all sorts of delightful things over the phone. It was a brand-new experience for me, and one that I will always remember.

Whatever happened to Rhonda? She is one of the girls I did track down recently. She has been happily married for twenty-plus years and has two children. And, although she has lost her Texas twang, she told me that many people do, indeed, tell her that she reminds them of Laura Bush. George W. and I could have done much worse.

Conclusion: For all practical purposes, Rhonda was just about perfect. Ultimately, I think that I just did not love her enough to marry her. You can't force it, and you can't fake it (love, that is). At least one of us is extremely happy and content—and I think that it is *her*.

Chapter Seven
The Man (And I Use That Term Very Loosely)

Gayle: The Nonstop Talker

Here I was, finally out of college and law school and actually earning a decent living. But since first grade, I had always been thrown together with girls in my various classes. In most years, finding a girlfriend was like shooting fish in a barrel. (At least I think that the phrase is "fish in a barrel." But why one would want to shoot fish in a barrel or shoot fish at all is beyond me.)

Now I was out in the real world. No more would there be first-, second-, or third-day-of-class girls. For that matter, no more would there be any-day-of-class girls. I was now completely on my own. Kinda scary, as I thought about it.

So I was thrilled when a fellow coworker fixed me up with Gayle. She was a cute, blonde-haired, blue-eyed Jewish girl (yes, you read correctly) from Long Island, New York, who sounded every bit like a Jewish girl from Long Island, New York, for good or ill.

Gayle was a sweet girl and meant well, but she never (and I do mean *never*) stopped talking. As Groucho would say, it was like she was "vaccinated with a phonograph needle." I liked her well enough to bring her to Dallas to meet the folks, and they liked her right away.

Still smarting from her experience with Stacey, my mom was on her best behavior and tried to say nothing but nice things. But even she pulled me aside after a few days and asked, "Doesn't she ever stop talking?" Sheepishly, I had to admit that, no, she did not. Needless to say, it was not a long-lasting relationship.

Conclusion: Nothing profound. She was a sweetheart in many ways. But I am a very quiet person by nature, and she was a nonstop talker. Never the twain shall meet. A relationship is a two-way street with two-way communication—an impossibility if one of the parties never, ever stops talking.

Marjie: The Redhead

I dated Marjie for about nine months or so. I had never dated a true redhead, and it was an eye-opening experience.

Marjie had all the qualities that one would associate with a redhead: temperamental, opinionated, dismissive, etc. She was a real handful and, frankly, quite challenging and fun for a while. But, ultimately, I concluded that my future lay elsewhere and ended it. And she quickly got married to the other beau in her life.

Over the years, she has reached out to me over the telephone and online from time to time. Apparently, her marriage was not a happy one, and I guess that she was looking for some warmth and compassion. However, I quickly realized that her personality had not changed in the least. Moreover, what

I found challenging and fun in a woman of twenty-five was merely tiresome in a woman of forty-five.

Accordingly, I have not encouraged her advances, and we will not be seeing each other again. However, I wish her all the happiness in the world.

Conclusion: Very simple. People do not/can not change their core personalities. So before you commit to a long-term relationship, make sure that you are doing so with someone you will be compatible with in the long run. If not, the relationship will, in all probability, not last.

Jodi: The Live-in Lover

When I met Jodi at a party, my first thought was that she was hot. My second thought was that she was an outrageous flirt. My third thought was that she truly did not like or respect men—at least that was the appearance she gave *vis-à-vis* the men I saw her flirting with at the party.

Unfortunately, that first thought was what led me to date her for two years—two very long years. However, in the end, that third thought, thank God, actually did save me from marrying her.

Jodi could be charming. As the saying goes, she was great for casuals. My parents met her and liked her, but she could never be a true friend or partner. Beware of any significant other who either puts you down in public, makes you the butt of her jokes, or both. Jodi did both.

In addition, I was very fortunate to meet her parents. Her mom was a real ball-buster (just like her), and her dad was a mild-mannered attorney (just like me). Hmm ... I just knew that, in twenty years' time, these two people would be *us*. It was very enlightening and very lucky for me that I was able to see it for myself, up close and personal.

Even after almost two years, with the relationship on its last legs, I thought that we'd give it another chance by moving in together. This was a big mistake, which led me to the following lessons learned.

Conclusion: Generally, a woman will turn into her mother, for good or ill. As I discussed with regard to Stacey, she will begin to look like her mother. As with Jodi, she will also begin to act like her mother. If you can't stand her mother, watch out. In addition, if her mother treats her father like crap, expect the same from her. And never move in together in the hopes that it will salvage a tottering relationship. It will never work. Finally, once you realize that a relationship is not working out, end it immediately. Don't stay in it an extra day longer, and certainly not months or years longer. Life is too short. Don't waste time.

Just one more thing ... Jodi was the first girl, to the best of my knowledge, who was not faithful to me. Winston Churchill once said that a man loves his friend because he or she stands by him at doubtful moments. It is obvious that Jodi never read Churchill, for she was certainly not one to stand by her man.

As I recall, I had just been operated on to correct a deviated septum. Jodi drove me back from the hospital, tucked me into bed to recover on my own, and went skiing for the weekend with "a friend." Such disregard and disrespect. It was very sad, really. So, as a result, I started an affair with ...

Melinda: The First Ballet Dancer

Melinda had been a principal dancer with the Colorado Ballet before injury put a halt to her career. She was young, adorable, and looked very much like Molly Ringwald. And, of course, I fell for her instantly.

Melinda also was from a very wealthy family. Her father, a prominent local attorney, hated my guts. Then again, I didn't feel too bad about it, as he had never even met me. I guess that he just didn't like the idea of an older guy dating his cherished younger, virginal (yeah, right!) daughter. To paraphrase Groucho in *Duck Soup*, "He was protecting her honor, which was more than she ever did."

Speaking of Molly Ringwald, I was a big fan of hers way back during her heyday. When she made the cover of *Time* magazine, I wrote to the editor of *Time* asking if she could be on the cover *every* week. I thought that request was very clever, as apparently did the editor, and my letter was published. But I never did hear from Molly, and she never made the cover of *Time* again. A coincidence? I'm not so sure.

Anyway, back to Melinda ... Unfortunately, she had all the problems one would associate with a ballet dancer: self-absorption, selfishness, anorexia, bulimia, and assorted other problematic behaviors. *Black Swan*, indeed. By the way, avoid all women who actually have a professional doctor's scale in their bathroom—a bad sign. (What can I say? I was getting back at Jodi.) Melinda also shared Jodi's attitude about being faithful.

The thing that stands out for me the most about Melinda is a phrase that I often read in Groucho's writings about Chico, which applied exactly to Melinda: she never failed to disappoint me in the fact that she would disappoint me. Did you follow that? If not, read that sentence again. I dodged a bullet, didn't I?

Melinda also seemed disdainful of my strong feelings for her. In the song by Berlin called "The Metro," there is a line which goes, "I remember hating you for loving me." Every time I heard that lyric, I would think of Melinda, as I really felt that she hated me for loving her. A bad sign.

People (actually, just men) have often asked me what it

is like to sleep with a ballet dancer. Well, all ballet dancers are different, as all attorneys are different. So one can't really generalize.

But the question reminds me of a *Seinfeld* episode where Jerry is dating a Romanian gymnast. He wants to break up with her before sleeping with her, as he just doesn't like her all that much. But Kramer talks him into it, as he wants to live vicariously through the delights that he believes Jerry is about to experience. After the deed is done, Jerry complains to Elaine that "it was just so *ordinary.*" That has been my experience as well.

Speaking of which, whenever Melinda and I would make love, we would both sweat profusely. I have never encountered that experience with any other lover. My best guess is that there was just something in our mutual body chemistries that caused such a reaction. But, to this day, I am at a loss as to why it always happened. I'll leave it to you doctors and chemists out there to figure it out and report back to me.

Conclusion: I guess that I said it all: self-absorption, selfishness, anorexia, etc. What was I thinking? One important lesson learned (once again!) was that you just can't help some people. Even if I was well equipped to help her with her issues, I am not at all sure that I could have succeeded. But I was not so equipped, and the end result would always be that she would drag me down to her level. Ultimately, surround yourself with mentally and spiritually healthy people, and you will be better off.

Sami: From France Nuyen to Yoko Ono

Yet another bullet dodged ... but I am getting ahead of myself.

People who know Sami now would never believe it, but

when I first met her she was quite beautiful in a France Nuyen sort of way. (Does anyone remember her? The movie *South Pacific*? Anyone?) Long dark hair, beautiful complexion, great figure, extremely bright (a CPA), and a lot of fun. I met her at an art auction, where she was prancing around and displaying the artwork and herself. She was quite charming, actually. But … that was then.

My downfall was in meeting her eighteen-month-old daughter, Katherine. Did you ever meet a child and fall instantly in love? I did so with Katherine. Hell, I even changed diapers. I must say that, to this day, some of the best times of my life were spent playing with that beautiful child. I know that you are way ahead of me here, but I continued the relationship with Sami for far too long, so that I would not lose the relationship with Katherine.

As I said, when I first met Sami, she seemed delightful. But, over time, she just became mean (or maybe she was always bitter, and I was just slow in realizing it). She came from a very strict household, and there did not appear to be a lot of affection between parents and siblings or between siblings. I noticed that right away and was bothered by it.

Sami's own household was very similar in all its negative aspects. She had a very troubled relationship with her older daughter, although she had a much better relationship with Katherine. Sami also shared with Jodi the trait of putting me down in public and making me the butt of her jokes. And as she became older and more bitter, France Nuyen morphed into Yoko Ono. (What was John thinking?)

Oh, well. At least I obtained personal financial advice, free of charge. For example, Sami twisted my arm to open up an IRA—sound financial advice. However, I would have gladly paid a professional for that advice in return for a number of years of my life back.

I made another terrible mistake. One of my oldest corporate clients was looking for a chief financial officer. I felt that Sami fit the bill, so I introduced them, and she was hired. One year later, she was fired for various and sundry reasons. She sued. I, quite rightly, recused myself. But I still followed the case as the attorney for the corporation and a potential witness.

Two years and many thousands of dollars in attorney's fees later, she lost the case. Justice was done, but I felt like I had been in a whirlpool of hate, lies, and deceit the entire time. Now, if clients are looking for an employee, I urge them to check out Monster.com.

Conclusion: More wasted years. Please, dear readers, never, ever stay in a relationship longer than good sense dictates. And never, ever stay in a relationship because of your fondness for the *kinder.* It does you no good, it does the mother no good, and it certainly does the child no good. It might be painful. It will be painful. But move on with your life. And, finally, never mix business with pleasure. Keep your girlfriend(s) and your client(s) separate and apart for all purposes. Never try to play "matchmaker" in that regard. You may end up losing both.

Michelle: The Rich Taiwanese Virgin

I had heard from a coworker that there was a young, attractive Asian woman (this was during my Asian phase) who worked in a local restaurant. Naturally, I went to check her out. We met, seemed to click, and began dating. I was still smooth back then.

Michelle was at least fifteen years younger than I was, and she was a virgin. She was from a fabulously wealthy family (her father owned many restaurants, including the one where we met) and lived with her parents and sisters in a palatial mansion. The inside of the house was filled with Chinese antiques and reminded me of one of the imperial palaces in the Forbidden City in Beijing. And, yes, I have been there.

I should have treated her home as a forbidden city, as her father seemed to have nothing but disdain for me. And I never even met the man—shades of Melinda here? I clearly remember walking up her driveway to introduce myself and shake his hand, and he did an about-face and headed back into the house. Talk about rejection.

Anyway, Michelle was crafty and seemed to like me, but, most of all, she wanted to lose her virginity. So she set up a situation whereby she seduced me in her second-floor bedroom. It was all very professionally done. And, in looking back on it, I give her great credit for her planning, except for the fact that the entire family was downstairs at the time. (I was scared to death!)

As I said, she was a virgin, and, as I alluded to in talking about Rhonda, only bed a virgin if you are truly in love with her and are willing to spend a great deal of time teaching her all the intricacies in matters sexual.

I enjoy teaching my clients about the law. I do not necessarily enjoy the other kind of teaching—personal preference. Everyone is different. However, I do not envy the Muslim terrorists who will find themselves with seventy virgins (or is it seventy-two virgins?) on their hands in Paradise. That sounds a bit more like hell than Paradise to me. That's just one Jew's opinion. *Shalom.*

Conclusion: Well, I have wracked my brain, but I cannot come up with any conclusions regarding my relationship with Michelle. So I will just wish her well and move on.

Marcella: The Artistic Street Urchin

Wow! Every guy should have a Marcella in his life at least one time or another ... or ... maybe not. After reading this story, you can decide for yourself. Let me know what you decide.

One day, I was eating at a Burger King (something that I try not to do too often), and, out of the corner of my eye, I saw a girl in another booth. She was a sweet, doe-eyed brunette and was very cute. She appeared to be filling out a job application, which told me that she was at least sixteen years old (perhaps a faulty assumption on my part). From her looks, she could have been twelve or twenty-four. It was hard to tell. As it turned out, she was eighteen years old. I was much older.

She completed her application and left. But to where? I made it my mission to try to find her and speak to her. This incident occurred in a strip mall, and I finally located her in a Hallmark store. I talked with her. We exchanged pleasantries and seemed to hit it off right away.

She told me that she was hungry, so we went back to my place. I made her a peanut butter and jelly sandwich, and we ended up in bed. (Apparently, I make a *mean* peanut butter and jelly sandwich.) I distinctly remember her asking me to tell her that I loved her, which I declined to do. My heart did go out to her. She seemed like a lost soul, and I was determined to help her out—mixed motives on my part.

Her story was as follows: she was from an affluent family from Philadelphia who had basically disowned her. She had just enough money to have an unfurnished apartment and pay for tuition at a local art school. Marcella was actually a brilliant artist. As for other necessities, like food, clothing, and art supplies, she had to beg, borrow, and steal (mostly steal). She was very street smart and was quite proud of the fact that she was able to pass for twelve years old so she could buy a child's bus pass.

Marcella was also very experienced in all matters sexual, and that was a big turn-on. She related to me that she had lost her virginity to another woman (!) at the age of twelve. I don't know if that was true, but she certainly did seem to know her way around the bedroom. She also liked to play games (like Daddy and Little Girl, etc.). Quite frankly, I thought that she was fascinating on a number of levels. But there was also a certain disconnect, as I was used to dating girls who could actually afford their own groceries and were not reduced to stealing.

How differently we thought about things is perfectly illustrated by the following story: I dropped by her apartment unannounced one night. Apparently, she was "entertaining" another boyfriend of hers named Lincoln (not "Abraham," I presume). Marcella was looking at me through the door's peephole and saw me reach into my back pocket. Immediately, she opened the door, fearing that I was reaching for a gun. A gun? Not only did I not own a gun, I wouldn't even know how to use one. I was actually reaching for my wallet to write her a note on one of my business cards. Talk about viewing the world from a different point of view!

I must admit that I kept Marcella to myself. I did not bring her when socializing with friends. I did not take her to any law firm functions, nor did I take her to places where I might run into other friends or coworkers. Could I have been ashamed of her? Possibly. I also would not allow her to be at my townhome in my absence. I could just picture returning to an empty house. Could I have not trusted her? Definitely.

It was not fated to last, but the relationship limped along for almost nine months ... although it was not exclusive, on either part, by any means. Then, just as suddenly as she appeared, she disappeared. That was probably a good thing. It was a fascinating experience, but one that I would not care to repeat.

Later, I heard through the grapevine that she got married and had two children. Good for her. I also heard that she became a devout Quaker. Honestly. No disrespect to Quakers, but I find that fact somewhat amusing. But, again, good for her.

Speaking of parents ... okay, I wasn't speaking of parents, but I will now. My late father was, and my mother still is, wonderful (part of "The Greatest Generation"). They retired to

Sarasota, Florida, after their children moved away from Dallas. Don't all parents live in Florida? I think that it is a federal law. (As for my parents, think Mr. and Mrs. Seinfeld ... don't think Mr. and Mrs. Costanza).

On occasion, I would envision my girlfriend *du jour* meeting the parents. I imagine getting off the plane with her, walking past the giant statue of De Soto at the Sarasota airport, and taking the escalator down to the baggage claim, where one of my parents would be waiting for us (the other would be standing by the car in the no-parking zone). I would get one of two reactions to my girlfriend.

The first reaction would be a sincere smile and a showing of happiness and approval. The second reaction would be a smile through gritted teeth, saying to her, "Nice to meet you," and then, in a private moment, I would get a dope-slap and the questions, "What are you thinking? Is this how we raised you?" These reactions would apply to both mom and dad equally.

Unfortunately, Marcella would have engendered reaction number two: the dope-slap reaction. No question about it. They would *not* have approved.

Conclusion: Very simple. If you care at all about what your parents think (and you should, to some extent), avoid those girls who would engender the dope-slap reaction. It's better for you, it's better for the girl, and it's better for your parents. Even if you don't care about what your parents think, it is still a good barometer to use in determining whether or not you should enter into or stay in a relationship.

Li (Meaning "Beautiful"): The Chinese Princess

I met Li in a restaurant, where she, like Michelle, was working as a waitress.

I have tried to hit on numerous hostesses and waitresses in

the past. There are some restaurants where I still can't show my face. Thank God there is a high turnover in these positions, so I am generally not banned for life.

Anyway, unknown to me, Li was not a poor immigrant waitress from China. She was going to the University of Denver and was working part time to alleviate boredom. She certainly did not need to work.

Indeed, not only was she one of the most beautiful women that I had ever met, but she was also from a very privileged background in China. Her father was a retired general in the Communist Chinese army, and she grew up in the former French embassy in Nanjing with servants, nannies, a driver, and so on. So much for communism in the People's Republic of China!

I often wondered what meeting the general would have been like. Would he have liked me, or would he have tried to cut my head off with his sword? Alas, I never got the opportunity to find out.

Li was also a successful businesswoman and a model, both in Denver and in China. In fact, she was my first and only calendar girl. She appeared on a calendar (fully clothed) in China. I thought that was so cool!

And, yes, I was in love with Li, and, for some reason, Li was also in love with me. There were certainly cultural differences and communication difficulties, but she was so sweet and kind that I did not feel that these posed insurmountable obstacles. (I even took Mandarin language lessons, but to no avail. I was hopeless!) We dated on and off for a number of years.

All that time, I pondered marriage with her. Sometimes, you can overanalyze matters. Just do it, as the Nike ads tell us. Finally, I summoned up the courage, bought an engagement ring, and prepared to ask her to marry me.

I had it all planned out in my mind. (That was one of my big mistakes.) I would get down on one knee, give her the ring, and propose. And she would hug me with tears in her eyes and say, "Yes, yes, of course, I will marry you!" That was the script in my mind, anyway.

The reality was that she looked at me, put the ring on, and said, "I'll think about it." I was crushed. Later, by the time that she was truly ready to accept, I had already met someone else.

Timing is everything in life. I don't know who first said that, but I won't be the last one to say it, nor will it be the last time that I say it. Did you follow that?

Of course, she kept the ring. Isn't it the law that the ring has to be returned if the marriage does not occur? At least that's what Judge Judy says. I get all my legal expertise from the television show *Judge Judy*—don't tell my clients. I'll have to research that issue more carefully.

Li and I have kept in touch over the years, but things could never be the same, especially now that she has permanently relocated to China. I still blame her for not saying yes. There are certain things that are out of our control. Maybe if I had been more persistent? Who knows? Speculation is useless at this point in time.

Conclusion: Again, don't waste precious time (a recurring theme here). Ask her to marry you sooner rather than later. If she says yes, great. If she says no, lick your wounds and move on. And always try to get the ring back—you can always find a willing buyer on eBay.

Afterthought on the TV show *Judge Judy*: This brief story will tell you the lengths that I have gone to with respect to meeting women. I was watching *Judge Judy* one evening and saw the most beautiful girl as a defendant on the show. I was so entranced by her that I wrote to the show's producers to see if I could get some information about her. Alas, there was no reply.

Akira: The Scary Geisha

As Li was spending more and more time in China, she decided that she would fix me up with someone so that I would not be lonely. I know. It sounded a bit suspect, but I went along with it anyway.

Her name was Akira. She was part-Chinese, part-Japanese, and very sexy. But she also was a bit coarse. And she was one tough cookie. She had been emancipated since the age of sixteen and had basically fended for herself since that time.

We got along fairly well, but she had a bad temper. She never got physically abusive, but you did not want to be around when she got angry. For example, one night I declined to have sex with her, and she threw me out of her apartment in a rage.

In retrospect, she reminds me of the beautiful, but evil, geisha played by Gong Li in the movie *Memoirs of a Geisha*. She even had a geisha outfit that she wore once in a while as a treat—for me. That was very sexy.

However, after more than a few months, I knew that I needed to get out of the relationship. But how could I break up with her without incurring her wrath and making her extremely A-N-G-R-Y? Well, that's where a good friend can come in handy.

I had known my friend Steve for a number of years. He was a handsome part-time actor. (We had appeared together in a *Perry Mason* made-for-television-movie.) He had met Akira and thought that she was attractive (and vice versa). So the three of us went out one night, and I made sure that, at the end of the night, she returned to his place instead of mine. Smooth. I felt like an NFL quarterback handing the football—Akira—off to a favorite halfback—Steve.

Soon thereafter I took a trip to Australia. When I arrived home, Steve and Akira picked me up at the airport. As they dropped me off at my house, I felt so *relieved* that I was going inside alone, and that Akira was driving off with Steve.

I wish I could say that Steve and Akira lived happily ever after. However, although they dated for quite some time, it was a very stormy relationship. But Steve was a big boy, so I didn't feel too bad about arranging for the transfer. However, one could say that it was a cowardly act of self-preservation. You decide.

Conclusion: Akira was the first girl I dated who had a scary temper. As soon as I encountered that temper, I should have walked out. However, I stayed for much longer than necessary and, therefore, had to put up with more temper tantrums than one man should have to endure. So, at the first sign of a bad temper, exit as gracefully and quickly as possible. And if you need to get in touch with Steve for assistance, please let me know.

Martell: A Sheryl Crow from the Other Side of the Tracks

Martell was a fix-up by one of my friends, a beautiful woman named Cyd. But more on Cyd in a moment.

Martell reminded me of Sheryl Crow. She had beautiful blonde hair, bright green eyes, and a smile that could light up a room. She was also intelligent and had a great sense of humor. And, yes, she was great in bed as well. (You knew that I would get around to that, didn't you?)

Sounds just about perfect, doesn't it? So what went wrong? Well, we were as different as night and day as far as our upbringing, likes and dislikes, and interests.

I grew up in an upper-middle-class environment, and my parents raised me to appreciate classical music, Broadway musicals, the theater, the ballet, classic old movies, etc. Martell grew up in a lower-middle-class environment and was never exposed to these things, and, therefore, she never enjoyed or appreciated them.

Whereas I would enjoy an old Fred Astaire/Ginger Rogers movie, an evening at the ballet, and a good glass of wine, Martell preferred the latest Batman movie, a monster truck rally, and a can of beer.

To Martell, these differences were amusing, and she liked to joke about them. To me, rightly or wrongly, they constituted a barrier to a long-standing relationship.

Conclusion: Mixed emotions. Would it have worked? Maybe. Should I have tried harder? Maybe. But in my own mind, I could never turn "maybe" into "yes," and so I moved on. And Martell had no problem moving on as well.

Afterthought on Cyd: Before Cyd fixed me up with Martell, Cyd and I dated for a brief time. But, ultimately, we just became good platonic friends, even though I continued to call her "Cydalicious."

One date in particular stands out in both our minds. We were sitting on the floor in my living room enjoying a good bottle of wine. At one point, I laid my head in Cyd's lap. And thinking that it would be a romantic gesture, she attempted to pour some wine into my mouth. Instead, it went up my nose, and I almost choked to death. Talk about waterboarding! Cyd and I still refer to that date as our "wine-up-the-nose" date.

Alisa: The Second Ballet Dancer

Like I said, every relationship should have a good first meeting story. This story is my best so far. I think that you'll like it, too.

I was still dating Li, on and off, and we had stopped at a

Blockbuster Video around 8:30 p.m. on a Saturday evening to rent a video. I was walking around the store, and suddenly I was mesmerized. Before me stood an Audrey Hepburn look-alike, circa 1953 (*Roman Holiday*). She was holding the video *The American President*, starring Michael Douglas—the movie that Li wanted to see. But there was only one copy. So this girl told us that we could have the video, as she had already seen the movie, and then she left.

I was beside myself. I didn't get a name, a type of car, or anything. Needless to say, I could not concentrate on Michael Douglas that evening. For the next three consecutive Saturdays, I showed up at Blockbuster Video at exactly 8:30 p.m. to see if I could find her. Nothing.

Slowly but surely, I forgot about her ... but not really. A few weeks went by, and I was jogging by my townhome complex one day, when across the street was this same girl walking a couple of dogs. I immediately went up to her and reminded her of our Blockbuster encounter. She did not recall it. I introduced myself, and she told me her name, Alisa. (Later, I would call her "The Little One" or "Pookie Pea.") I gave her my business card and told her to call me if she ever wanted to get together for sushi. (I thought that the offer of sushi would sound sophisticated!)

As it turned out, she was house- and dog-sitting for a neighbor of mine. I was obsessed. I had to think of something cute to do to get her attention, so I bought the movie *Funny Face* (starring a very *young* Audrey Hepburn and a very *old* Fred Astaire) and left it at my neighbor's door with a card and photo asking her to call me. Nothing.

Months went by, and I didn't see her again until the next summer. I was shopping at my local Safeway, and she passed by. At least, I thought that it was her. Young girls can change a lot from year to year, and I had no idea how old she was (twenty years old as it turned out). I told myself that I would pick up one more grocery item and then go talk to her. But by the time

I did so, she was gone. I searched the Safeway aisles for an hour. Again, nothing.

A week later, I was sweeping out my garage, and she drove by. Coincidence? Karma? Kismet? Stalking? I didn't know, but I did take down her license plate number, went to the Colorado DMV office, and got her name and address. (Please note, you can no longer do that in the State of Colorado under what, I believe, they call "The Barry Law.")

Well, I wrote to her again, enclosing another photo. She did call, we went out that same evening, and we dated for the next four years. I wish that I could say it was four years of bliss.

There were danger signs. Alisa was a ballet dancer and, unfortunately, somewhat self-absorbed. My first clue came upon entering her apartment. She had framed photos of herself everywhere I looked. Later, there was another danger sign. She had lied to her mother that she was still attending college, and so she was receiving tuition money from mom but spending it on ballet lessons and other assorted living expenses. Another danger sign came when I asked her if she ever wanted children, and she said, "No, because I never want anyone to treat me the way that I treat my mother."

Finally, I never felt totally secure in the relationship. I always felt that if, God forbid, I should get sick, lose my job, etc., she would be gone. I felt that very strongly, and nothing that she ever did caused me to change my mind or rethink that potential problem. This is not a good sign for a healthy long-term relationship. But I was in love with her, so I noted but chose to ignore all of these signs and potential problems. As they say, love is blind. And as Dandy Don Meredith once said, "they" is a very reliable source.

However, I always thought that we looked good together as a couple. Of course, I may have been mistaken in that assumption. One evening after one of Alisa's ballet performances, a patron came up to me and congratulated me on how well my *daughter* danced. Ouch!

Alisa was wonderful in a hundred different ways, and we had many interests in common, such as the ballet, the theater, opera, classical music, movies, fine food, and the like. But, over time, our relationship developed into a quasi-platonic relationship. I still loved her and—don't tell anyone—probably still do to this day. However, I think that I also started taking her and the relationship for granted. This was a big mistake in many ways.

As I said, after four bittersweet years, it was over. Alisa had just been accepted to attend the Kirov Academy of Ballet in Washington, DC, which was a great honor. (Okay, so we fudged her age a bit on the application—sue me.) Of course, she could not afford the tuition, so I, the altruistic and by now ex-boyfriend, Barry, paid her tuition for a year hoping that, at the end of the year, she could audition for ballet companies from all over the world. Unfortunately, she injured herself during the audition period, and her ballet career was over. In retrospect, I think that I may have wanted a ballet career for Alisa more than she wanted it for herself.

We never saw each other again. In fact, she never even thanked me. No good deed goes unpunished. I am afraid that statement is as true today as it was when it was first uttered all those many years ago. Oh, well.

The good—nay, great—news ... I got custody of our perfect black cocker spaniel puppy, Zorro, who was the light of my life until his untimely passing. So very sad.

Conclusion: No girl is perfect. No relationship is perfect. And in this case, there were certainly danger signs and potential pitfalls. But if the girl/relationship is important enough to you, never, ever take either for granted. Keep conscious of not doing so every day. If you love her, let her know it, in ways large and small, every single day. I know that it sounds easy, but it is actually quite difficult. But do try—you will thank me. I just wish that I had done so. Where were you, dear reader, when I needed your advice?

Afterthought on The Little One: In reading and rereading this section on The Little One, it occurred to me that relationships are full of contradictions. On the one hand, I loved her with all my heart; on the other hand, I was fairly certain that we could not build a life together. In retrospect, I should have gone with what my heart told me and worked hard at making the relationship a success.

Emily: The Exotic Dancer

I was in the habit of frequenting a very nice Japanese restaurant near my home, and I became friendly with the manager. The manager was a very creative marketer for the restaurant. For example, she had asked all single patrons for their photos and decreed that every Wednesday night would be singles night.

I was not really interested in participating in singles night, but I did give her a photo. Later, she showed me a photo of a very attractive blonde who wanted to meet me. I took her name and number and called her.

Her name was Emily, and she was, by her own description, an "exotic dancer." Where I grew up, we would have called her a "stripper." She had aspirations for a music career and likened herself to Gwen Stefani—no way. There was nothing terribly interesting or exciting about Emily, I promise. Suffice it to say, she was very sexy, but a bit coarse and uneducated. I wasn't seeing anyone else at the time, so I continued to see Emily.

One date particularly stands out in my mind. Emily had me take her to a store specializing in "adult" products and wanted me to buy dog collars for the both of us. Idiot that I was, I meekly complied. They were both black felt collars surrounded by rhinestones. I never asked her what they were for—frankly,

I did not want to know. In any event, we never did anything with the collars, and the relationship ended shortly thereafter. But I had a perfect use for mine: Zorro looked so handsome in *his* new collar!

Our last date was also somewhat memorable. I had been invited by friends, the owners and operators of a local ballet academy, to a charity benefit for their ballet school. As the only person I was seeing at the time was Emily, I brought her with me, hoping against hope that she would not do or say anything to humiliate me. While she didn't quite fit in (to put it mildly), I survived the evening with my dignity intact.

As an aside, I do recall that she wore a very short skirt to the event. I remember that the men (mostly husbands) at the event kept looking at her with lust in their eyes, while the women (mostly wives) in the room stared daggers at her. It was a very interesting dynamic.

The relationship having run its course, we stopped seeing each other. I am sure that neither of us grieved about the end of our relationship.

Conclusion: Simple. As with a number of women that you have already met or will shortly meet, I was loathe to introduce Emily to family, friends, or coworkers. Avoid all such women who might become an embarrassment. You will know who they are instinctively. Follow your instincts.

Olga: The Last, and Certainly Least, Ballet Dancer

As it turned out, my friends at the ballet academy were none too impressed with Emily and decided that they would fix me up with one of their dancers, named Olga, a cute Siberian girl. What they should have realized was that Olga was not a big (or even a small) improvement over Emily. God bless them. I am sure that they meant well, but Olga was a walking (or dancing) disaster.

As I said, Olga was a cute girl. She was a wisp of a girl with blonde hair, blue eyes, and a ballet dancer's body.

But she was in this country illegally, and she cleaned houses to make ends meet. As all of her money was made under the table, she paid no taxes. Whatever money she did earn, she gambled away on trips to Las Vegas. In addition, Olga spoke English very poorly, was not at all interested in improving her language skills, and had a dour Siberian personality.

If that wasn't quite enough to put a man off, she had gray teeth. (A doctor friend of mine told me that, in the former countries of the Soviet Union, they used to treat children with tetracycline, which would turn their teeth gray from the inside out, so teeth-whitening would not be an option.) While my heart goes out to Olga and those like her, I must admit that when I was not in her company, I affectionately referred to her as "Gray Tooth." (Kind of like "Braveheart"—okay, maybe not like it at all.) People have asked me, "Did you kiss her?" I have sheepishly admitted that, "Yes, I did." I know, I know.

Frankly, even a few years ago, I would not have given her the time of day, but one gets lonely, desperate, and (you fill in the blank) at times. I set out to warm her cold Siberian heart, but it was not meant to be. It was a relationship in name only. Against my better judgment, I tried to make it work. She did absolutely nothing to further the relationship.

Our last night together was on a Christmas Day evening. I gave her wonderful presents, which were not reciprocated. She cooked me an inedible Russian meal. We agreed not to see each other again and—"Merry Christmas"—we never did see each other again.

A few months later, she had remarried (her second marriage), and within six months she was divorced again. Two marriages and divorces before the age of thirty—a future Siberian Elizabeth Taylor (*with gray teeth*) in the making.

The near-relationship with Olga reminds me of what can result from desperation and lowering one's standards. Have you ever driven home after a night of clubbing and, having failed to meet anyone, started looking into the windows of cars next to you for that one last possible pickup? To me, that was Olga. But it could also apply to any of a number of girls whom I may have met and spent a brief amount of time with over the years. And, yes, Olga would definitely have engendered the dope-slap reaction from my parents, as discussed above with respect to Marcella.

Conclusion: Whatever you do, don't ever lower your standards just to be with someone. It is much better to be alone. I was lucky. I lowered my standards to be with Olga for a mere six months or so. It was misguided and stupid, but I have known others who have lowered their standards for a lifetime of misery. Be smart. To the Olgas of the world, just say "*Nyet!*"

Kelly: The Felon

Okay, okay, she wasn't really a felon, but she was too close for my comfort—much too close.

When I first met her, she seemed intelligent (notice how I started off with that one?) and charming, with a pretty face and a very nice figure. I even took her to my law firm's Christmas party that year, and she seemed to fit in just fine, with no embarrassments.

She specifically told me (or at least led me to believe) that she was gainfully employed at a bank, that she had never been married, and that she had no children. The subject of a criminal record never came up in our initial conversations. (Should it be mandatory?)

But almost every single time that I got together with her, her story would change. She actually did not work at a bank, but had only started an apprentice-type program. Later, she was no longer working at the bank as an apprentice, as the bank had discovered her criminal record. (Yikes! What criminal record?) Her first story was that an ex-boyfriend had failed to pay a cab driver, and she had been charged with theft. Well, that didn't sound quite right. Her next story was that it had to do with some type of domestic-relations offense. I didn't want to know any more and figured that I would never get at the complete truth anyway.

Still later, I learned that she had been married and had a teenage son that her mother had raised from infancy. The truth? You tell me. In any event, it really didn't matter, as there had been too many lies, too much negative information, and all too soon. I decided that I had to stop seeing her, and I did stop. That was the end of Kelly ... or so I thought.

A few months later, I got a call from a "girlfriend" of hers asking me to bail her out of jail. The story from her friend was that she had been jailed for a traffic offense. As I was no longer seeing her, I declined the kind invitation. After Kelly got out of jail, she called me. Apparently, her "girlfriend" was her former cellmate (!), and Kelly explained that she had been unfairly jailed after an altercation at a bar—yet another story.

Kelly was upset with me for not helping her to get out of jail. But we had dinner one more time—don't ask me why—and I never saw her again. Of course, I am not an avid watcher of the TV show *Cops*, so I may have missed more of her shenanigans.

Conclusion: When one lie rears its ugly head, there are usually more waiting in the wings. Be wary, be diligent, and if it turns out that she does have a criminal record, don't even think twice about ending it—whether or not you are an attorney.

Chapter Eight
The Good, the Bad,
and the Miscellaneous

Brenda: The Hawaiian Affair

After my graduation from college, my father treated my family (my mother, sister and then brother-in-law, and me) to a week trip to Hawaii. I was anxious to go, but I also felt like the proverbial fifth wheel, so I was hoping to meet someone there.

We took a direct flight from Dallas to Honolulu, and I noticed on our flight an adorable girl with short blonde hair, a winsome smile, and a cute figure. Apparently she was with a friend and her mother. Yes, I was eavesdropping just a bit. I didn't make any moves during the flight, as I just knew that, after the plane landed, we would go our separate ways.

Thank God I was wrong, as we both checked into the Hilton Hawaiian Village Hotel on Waikiki Beach. That first night we met, and it was lust at first sight. Her name was Brenda, and she was from Ida, Louisiana. I was twenty-two, she was seventeen, and not yet being an attorney, I knew nothing about statutory rape or even if it applied in this instance—which I doubt. *Aloha*, Brenda.

I was staying in my parents' room, and even though they got suspicious when my mom found Brenda's slippers under my bed one afternoon, they didn't mind. They liked Brenda, and she became part of our family for the remainder of the trip. What a grand time!

This was the era of sex, drugs, and rock and roll, especially on a Hawaiian trip, and I am afraid Brenda and I indulged in the first two quite extensively. Have you ever had sexual activity on Waikiki Beach at 3:00 a.m.? Well, Waikiki Beach is never deserted at any time of the day or night. I don't know how I had the nerve, but it was that kind of time, and Brenda was that type of companion. The week went by too quickly in a haze of sex, drugs, swimming, touring, eating, and just having the time of my life. As with all good things, it ended all too quickly.

Thankfully, Brenda was on the flight back to Dallas, so we could say our good-byes. We were seated by ourselves in those double seats that are always in the middle of the plane on jumbo jets. We covered our laps with blankets, and she said good-bye to me in the nicest way that she could. At one point, my dad came by to see how we were doing. "Just fine, Dad. Please leave." No, Brenda and I didn't quite join the Mile High Club, but we came close. (A bad pun? I'm not so sure.)

Conclusion: No conclusion here—just memories of a very nice girl and very exciting times. I wish you all a Brenda and a romantic trip to Hawaii. But do remember that holiday romances are not real romances. Do not ever confuse the two. I would learn that lesson all too clearly in time.

Crystal and the X-Rated Movies

I met Crystal while she was working part time as a waitress at an athletic club that I frequented. Her other part-time job was at a video store that promoted X-rated movies. She was blonde, cute, and willing. I was brunette, cute, and willing. And so we began dating.

But I must admit that most of our dates took the form of dinner at a restaurant and then back to her place to watch a movie. And I remember that we never got more than ten or fifteen minutes into a movie before we ended up in the bedroom.

At the time, it seemed like great fun. But, in retrospect, it all seems a bit tawdry. And as quickly as she entered into my life, she left it. I am sure that neither of us grieved the loss of the other.

Conclusion: As I said, it all strikes me now as rather tawdry. And I knew for a fact that she was not exclusive. I am sure that she had many happy moviegoers to her credit. So, frankly, I should have just passed on the whole experience and rented exclusively from Blockbuster.

Joan: My Very First Cougar

Joan was a pretty and petite brunette. And she was my very first cougar. I was twenty-four at the time, and she was thirty-six. And, although the term was not yet in use, she was a cougar. In retrospect, I was too young for her, and she was too old for me. But we got along well, and so we dated for a few months or so.

Frankly, I don't remember too much about the relationship. However, two things do stand out in my mind.

The first centered around the loss of her father. He had recently passed away, and she was terribly shaken when she saw him in his coffin. She specifically told me to make sure that I saw a dead body before I saw a relative in his/her coffin. That advice has always stayed with me. It is funny how we remember certain things all of our lives that are said to us even if they are said to us by people who are not necessarily integral in our lives. But I always remembered what she told me and made it a point to attend funerals and to look at the deceased anytime that there was an open casket.

Years later, my own father passed away, and I was able to kiss him on the forehead and say good-bye. It was terribly sad, but I might not have been able to do so had I not heeded Joan's warning all those many years ago.

The second thing that comes to mind centered on her upcoming birthday. I wanted to get her something really nice, so I went shopping at the mall. Well, I am ashamed to say it, but I ended up getting her a stuffed animal. Mind you, it was a quite large and beautiful stuffed animal of a horse. But it was a stuffed animal all the same. I should have realized that a grown woman would prefer jewelry, perfume, or anything other than a stuffed animal. But it was my immaturity that was showing itself.

Needless to say, Joan was very disappointed in my present, and in me. And she broke up with me shortly thereafter. I can't say that I blamed her. I realized at the time that she needed someone older and more mature. And, frankly, I was a bit disappointed in myself. But life goes on, and we both went on to other relationships.

Conclusion: No great insights here. I guess that I was just a very young twenty-four-year-old, and Joan needed a more mature man. But I must admit that I still like giving stuffed animals as presents. However, I am also sure to supplement such gifts with more mature and meaningful gifts.

Gayle and Michelle: The Last of the Cougars

I was in my late twenties when I met Gayle and Michelle, who were both fully ten years older than me. Just think—they are either collecting Social Security or dead by now. A scary thought! In any event, they were my last cougars. But that was all that they had in common.

Gayle was a former model from Chicago and had been a gorgeous redhead. But time had not been kind to her looks. She was still living off her modeling income and seemed to have little enthusiasm for life or sex.

Michelle, on the other hand, was a very attractive Irish lass with dark hair and beautiful green eyes. She was also very intelligent and had a responsible professional occupation. And she was very good in bed.

As I look back on it, I am not sure why I didn't stop dating Gayle and just concentrate on Michelle. But I was young and immature at the time and so just remained passive and continued to see them both.

Ultimately, Gayle just faded away, but my youth and immaturity drove Michelle away. I can't blame her. She needed a mature man in her life, and I was still just a boy in many ways. I just wish that we had been closer in age and, therefore, may have had a chance.

Conclusion: Timing is everything in life. Michelle needed me to be the mature man that I most assuredly was not at the time. And there is nothing that anyone could have done about it. I just hope that she did find such a man. And, knowing her as I did, I am sure that she did find him.

Nicole: Miss Sarasota ... Almost

Recently, I was at Siesta Beach on Siesta Key in Sarasota, Florida, when flashbacks of Nicole entered my head.

I was visiting my parents in Sarasota and wanted to return home with a Florida tan. I had just spent the entire day at Siesta Beach. I was fried to a crisp and was about to leave when I saw a vision of loveliness pass by.

She was a beautiful, buxom brunette, and she was wearing a skimpy bikini. I grabbed a towel, flung it over my head (looking very much like Omar Sharif in *Lawrence of Arabia*), and began to walk beside her.

As she walked by, all eyes (male and female) turned toward her and me as I was walking by her side. Well, the best line that I could come up with at the time was, "Are these people staring at you or me?" Not bad. But, more importantly, *she* thought that it was very funny.

So we got to know each other. She was not only lovely, but very sweet as well. Her name was Nicole, and she was competing in the Miss Sarasota contest that coming weekend. But, unfortunately, I was leaving the next day. There was just no opportunity to spend some quality time with her. I wished her luck, we exchanged information, and I hoped to further the relationship somehow.

Nicole did not win. She came in third, which was still pretty impressive. And we continued to communicate for a few months. But it did not work out, as our communication abruptly ceased, and I never saw her again.

A short time after our communication ended, my mom sent me her engagement announcement from the Sarasota *Herald-Tribune*. I was disappointed, but I couldn't help thinking that the bridegroom was one fortunate guy!

I don't know whatever became of Nicole, but I think of her every time that I take a stroll on Siesta Beach.

Conclusion: Sometimes, you just have to go for it. What is the worst that can happen? You will be rejected. *Big deal!* Take the risk. There is nothing worse than a lost opportunity. No, it ultimately did not work out with Nicole. But I gave it the old college try, and I can live with that.

Gitta and the Aborted Three-Way

Gitta was an interesting girl. She was a tall, brunette, full-bodied German girl with an insatiable desire for sex.

She once told me that she practiced her oral sex technique on a cucumber. I found that fact then, and still find it now, a rather odd confession. But I guess that everyone must have a hobby. And, frankly, I think that it probably did improve her technique. We dated for a few months, and, in that time, I got to know her best friend, whose name escapes me.

One day Gitta proposed that we invite her friend to join us in our lovemaking. And, in a decision much regretted by my male friends who have heard this story, I politely declined. Frankly, I wasn't physically attracted to her friend and just didn't like her all that much. And I felt, rightly or wrongly, that if I took on such an assignment, then I would want to do the very best job that I could and dive into the action, so to speak, with all my heart and soul. And, to be honest, I just couldn't do it.

Gitta was upset and disappointed, and it brought our relationship to an abrupt end. Frankly, I was a bit surprised. I guess that I just hadn't realized how important it had been to her. Such is life.

Conclusion: No regrets whatsoever. Meeting and getting to know Gitta was a pleasure. But I still don't think that I would have enjoyed an additional playmate added to the mix. And, yes, I can hear my male readers letting out a collective groan with respect to my decision. But I *still* made the right decision—for me.

The Hispanic Telemarketer

Have you ever been so lonely or desperate for female companionship that you began flirting with anonymous telephone operators or telemarketers? Well, I did ... just once.

As I mentioned, I graduated from the University of Denver College of Law. One evening, I received a call from a girl working as a telemarketer for the DU Alumni Association. I don't remember how it happened, but we seemed to hit it off. One thing led to another, she came over after her shift, and we made love. Yes, it's a bit bizarre, even for me.

I don't remember much about her other than she was Hispanic, she was attractive, and she was my first partner to sport a tattoo. I don't even remember her name, but I do remember her calling me again and my making it clear to her that it was a one-time thing. It was during my immature "love 'em and leave 'em" period, which is amply reflected in this chapter.

She was such a nice girl that, in retrospect, I wish I had given her at least half a chance. I guess that I was just too wrapped up in meeting and mating too many women.

Conclusion: One-night stands are clearly overrated if, indeed, anyone rates them highly at all. I guess that they are a part of an active dating life. But may I suggest good books, movies, or dog walks as much better substitutes? Believe me, spiritually speaking, those substitutes are much healthier.

Afterthought on desperation: I once even tried to hit on a homeless girl. She was a cute young thing. And she was standing at an intersection with a sign stating that she was homeless and hungry. So I went to a fast-food joint and bought her a burger and fries. I also gave her my business card and asked her to call me. (And, yes, she did have a cell phone. She was purportedly homeless, but she *still* had a phone.) Anyway, she was very grateful for the meal, but she never called. In retrospect, she was probably not homeless at all. In fact, she probably earned more than I did. Not a bad gig!

Elizabeth: The Drinker

Elizabeth—dear, beautiful, troubled Elizabeth. She could have walked into the Playboy headquarters and become an instant centerfold. She was *that* attractive.

Elizabeth was a dark-haired goddess (picture Vivien Leigh in *Gone with the Wind*) with a "form like mortal sin." (I got that great line from Katharine Hepburn as Eleanor of Aquitaine in *The Lion in Winter*.) Anyway, Elizabeth was almost perfect in every way. To quote Homer, she was a "queen of soft desire." (You didn't think that I could quote Homer, did you?)

Unfortunately, she had a problem with alcohol—at least it appeared so to me. She reminds me of the old joke: "Does she drink? Yes, but only to excess." That was Elizabeth.

I met her when she was temping as a receptionist for a law firm that I once worked for. Repeat after me: never date a coworker. It could be disastrous on a whole number of different levels. More on that a little later.

Our first date was a casual dinner date. I knew that something was wrong when she had downed three mixed drinks before we finished our appetizers. Things went downhill from there. Did I learn a lesson? No.

Our second date was to see the movie *Pinocchio*. Before the movie began, she said that she had to go to the restroom, and she never came back. Later, the next day, she told me that she had run into some friends and went out partying with them. Strange, but did I finally learn a lesson? No.

Our third and last date occurred on a very cold and icy New Year's Eve. She was wearing a slinky dress that showed off all her curves to great advantage, but I was still very wary. I put my foot down and decreed that she was to have only one mixed drink before the dinner portion of our meal.

I knew that I had lost the battle after she had downed her *fourth* drink before dinner actually arrived. We got through dinner at about 10:00 p.m., and I felt that I needed to get her home ASAP. Have you ever struggled to navigate a drunken woman in three-inch stiletto heels over an icy parking lot?

I finally got her into the car, and I was so disoriented by then that I asked her for directions to her home. She told me, but I felt that she was in no condition to give me accurate directions, so I flagged down a cop and asked him for directions. He basically repeated her directions, and then … wham … Elizabeth smacked me right across the face. Apparently, she was furious that I hadn't listened to her directions. I was just stunned. By that time, I just wanted the night to end and to go home.

When we arrived at her place, she invited me inside and, against my better judgment, I went in. In minutes, we were making love. A mistake? You bet. In the middle of the act, she reared back her legs and donkey-kicked me across the room. I was again stunned and speechless.

She then put on her nightgown and began brewing a pot of hot coffee, probably thinking that it would be a long night. Whatever she was thinking, I was thinking that I really needed to get the hell out of there before I was drenched with a pot of scalding hot coffee. So I told her that I had to leave.

She looked at me, coyly pulled up her nightie, and asked, "Don't you want more of this?" In my best Woody Allen impersonation, I said, "Well, it looks very nice, but I'm double-parked, and I've got to feed my goldfish, so I really should be getting home." Within the next hour, I was home safe and sound in my own bed, alone. I considered myself very lucky.

I saw Elizabeth one more time. She was tending her garden and told me that she was on the wagon. I hope, for her sake, that she stayed there—otherwise, what a waste.

Conclusion: Elizabeth was my first, and last, experience with someone who drank a great deal. And, of course, I was, and still am, a lightweight when it comes to alcohol. But if you find yourself involved with a person who drinks a great deal, I wish you the best of luck. My very limited experience is that there is nothing that you can do for the other person unless that person wants to stop drinking. If that person doesn't want to stop, you either have to leave or commit yourself to a life sentence of anguish and despair. Good luck.

Sandy: The Receptionist

Have I mentioned that you should never date a coworker? Have I ever followed my own advice? You be the judge (and jury).

Her name was Sandy, and she was a very sweet girl with light brown hair and a beautiful smile. She was also quite a good receptionist at one of my prior law firms.

I believe that Sandy had just gotten engaged to be married. We never talked about it, but I think that she wanted one last fling before matrimony. Not that I minded, but, as I recall, it was not my idea. Not that it matters.

During that very brief affair, we found ourselves alone in the office at 5:00 p.m. one afternoon. All the other attorneys were elsewhere, and all the staff had just gone home. One thing led to another, and we found ourselves in the sixth-floor stairwell enjoying the solitude of the building by making love. I felt fairly secure about not being interrupted, as it was a six-floor building.

What I found out later, and what she apparently knew, was that there was a seventh floor where all the janitorial personnel had their offices, so getting caught was a real possibility. I often wondered whether she kept that information from me, knowing that I would never have gone with her if I had known. I guess I'll never know the answer to that question.

Sandy did, indeed, get married. I went to the wedding. I always feel odd going to a wedding where I have slept with the bride. It is a strange experience on so many different levels. In any event, I hope that it worked out for her.

Conclusion: Take my advice. Never have sexual relations with anyone in the workplace. It is a bad idea for a number of reasons. Chiefly, a sexual-harassment lawsuit can ruin you professionally and financially—a very good reason, indeed, for listening to this attorney. Now, if I would only listen to my own advice, everything would be fine. But as the saying goes, an attorney who represents himself or herself has a fool for a client.

Lera: The Office Manager and the Chinese Fire Drill

Have I mentioned that … Okay, I guess that I have mentioned it. Same law firm, different employee—no wonder that this law firm is no longer in existence!

Lera was a pretty blonde Southern girl with a charming Southern accent and great legs. She was our office manager and was also having an affair with the senior partner of the firm, whom I will call Bob, because that was his name.

Lera and I had "been together" only a couple of times. She was the only girl that I've ever been with who actually lit up a cigarette after sex—a big turnoff. Anyway, back to our story.

It was a hot April afternoon, and I just dropped in on Lera after work. It was about 5:45 p.m., and she was getting ready to go to the theater with Bob. He was to pick her up at 6:00 p.m., but Lera wanted a "quickie," so we engaged.

During that brief moment of passion, one of my eyes was on Lera, and the other was on the clock. I finished at about 5:50 p.m., leaving Lera completely unsatisfied. I had to get the hell out of there, so by 5:55 p.m., I had sneaked out the back stairwell, yelling to Lera behind me that she could come over later if she wanted.

I left without Bob seeing me. I felt that I had survived with my job intact and just wanted to go home to the peace and serenity of my house. Little did I know what was in store for me.

I went home, and Melinda stopped by. One thing led to another, and we ended up in bed. All of a sudden (it was about 9:00 p.m.), I heard a pounding on my front door. It was Lera, her hormones raging. At the same time, the phone rang, and it was Jodi (my current live-in lover) calling from out of town.

So, here I was: Melinda in bed, Lera pounding on the door, and Jodi on the phone. Grand Central Station was never busier. It was like a Marx Brothers movie or a Three Stooges short. (Call me Shemp!) So what did I do? I didn't answer the door. I got off the phone. And I showed Melinda the door. Whew!

I don't relate this story with any amount of pride or satisfaction. In fact, it sort of makes me feel a bit disgusted with myself. I felt the same way at the time. But since I am trying to relate all stories that may be of some interest, this one deserves its place alongside the others.

Did I learn anything from this episode? Yes. Don't be such a goddamned pig! Maybe I am being too hard on myself, but it certainly wasn't one of my finest hours.

Conclusion: A "Chinese fire drill" is defined as a state of utter confusion. I tend to be a bit of an anal-compulsive. Utter confusion in any aspect of my life is anathema to me, but utter confusion in my love life is the worst. If you are like me, avoid it at all costs.

Vanessa: My African American Girlfriend

Vanessa was a very beautiful girl, an astute businesswoman, and a loving mother to her young daughter. And, frankly, I liked her a lot.

We dated for only about three or four months, and I can't remember why we stopped seeing each other. She was just one of the many women that I let slip through my fingers, so to speak.

But what I remember most about Vanessa was the reactions that we would get from other people. I have dated Asian and Hispanic women and never noticed reactions of any kind from third persons. But it was different with Vanessa, an African American girl.

Whenever Vanessa and I went out in public together, people would look up and stare at us. This reaction would happen equally at restaurants, stores, movie theaters, and other public places. I thought then, and still think to this day, that it was because I was a white man, and she was a black woman. And it angered me that people were looking at us just because we had different skin colors.

We never discussed it, but I am sure that Vanessa probably had to put up with such reactions all her life. And so she was either immune to it, or at least she did not let it bother her. But I noticed it right away, and it bothered the hell out of me. So it was not fated to last.

Conclusion: As I stated earlier, Vanessa was a wonderful woman. I just couldn't get past the prejudice that I encountered when I was with her. So I just chalked it up to a bittersweet experience and moved on. And I was content with that decision.

Angelina: The Hairstylist

She was my new hairstylist. (Now I just get haircuts—they are cheaper. And, yes, I still have my hair!)

Anyway, Angelina was cute, young, and interested. Do you see a pattern here? Actually, she reminded me of the thin Kirstie Alley, from *Cheers*. Very sexy, indeed.

We started dating, but we really had nothing in common. In fact, she was a bit common in her interests and attitudes, and she didn't care for sex. She claimed that she had been raped at sixteen years of age and, therefore, didn't like sex. I was actually quite understanding about it, believe it or not. We did engage in sex, but it was always rather brief and unemotional. And after a short period of time, I stopped seeing her, as I just didn't feel a great connection.

Fast-forward four years ... I was not dating anyone and was starting to think about Angelina. I convinced myself that I had not been very nice to her, that I had not given the relationship a chance, and so on. I did some research and located her. She was now styling hair in North (or South?) Carolina. I called her, and we arranged for her to come to Denver to visit me.

This decision was a big mistake. Within the first minute of being with her, I remembered why I had broken up with her in the first place. We had nothing in common. There was no connection. She was, if anything, even more common than when I had known her. The next couple of days seemed like an eternity, but at last she was gone.

Conclusion: Thomas Wolfe once wrote, "You can't go home again." Well, he could just as easily have said, "You can't resurrect an old relationship again." An old relationship is like Humpty Dumpty after the fall. A word to the wise: never try to resuscitate an old relationship. It doesn't work the second time around. With the possible exception of Robert Wagner and

Natalie Wood (poor Natalie!), I have never heard of it working. So don't waste your time.

Jennifer: The Vamp

We literally met as we were passing each other in traffic. That is, for some reason, our eyes locked as she passed me in her car. Of course, I did an immediate U-turn and began my pursuit. She parked her car at a Planned Parenthood facility and went in. I did not follow, but I left a note with my business card and placed it on her windshield.

She called. I never asked her about her trip to Planned Parenthood, but we got along well enough on the phone to arrange a meeting. Jennifer was young and not particularly well educated, but she had beautiful blonde hair and exquisite, bright blue eyes—at the time, a good substitute for higher education.

Jennifer was a bit of a flirt and a big tease. She used to stare at me with those big, beautiful eyes and say that she was "vamping" me with her eyes. I wish that she had vamped me with other parts of her body, but she was resistant to anything other than making out. Frustrating.

Jennifer also loved to shop and would always take me with her to Victoria's Secret, where she would try on lingerie. Unfortunately, she never left the dressing room or invited me in to see her dressed in that sexy lingerie. *Very* frustrating.

Ultimately, we had very little in common, and the relationship was going nowhere, so I stopped seeing her.

It was only after a couple of years had passed that she got in touch with me again. She had gotten pregnant with someone whom she was no longer seeing. I didn't ask her what she wanted from me, but just told her that I was busy. Thereafter, every few months, I would hear from her inquiring whether or not I was seeing anyone. Even if I was not seeing anyone, I always told her that I was. Eventually she got the hint and stopped calling.

Conclusion: There are some girls whom you will never be able to figure out. I could never figure out what Jennifer was up to or what she wanted from me. Maybe she didn't even know herself. In any event, it did not matter, as you can't build a relationship on a flimsy, or nonexistent, foundation. In retrospect, I should have just kept on driving.

Audrey: The Teutonic Beauty

I met Audrey at a local tennis center where we both played. I think that I fell in love with her from the first moment that I saw her. She was blonde with a beautiful face and athletic figure. She was also quick-witted, and we began bantering from the moment we met—a big turn-on.

She was very close to her parents and was living with them for the summer before she began working toward her master's degree at Harvard (of all places), so I got to know her parents very well. They were both from Germany, grew up during World War II, and still had much of the old country in their veins. They spoke German for the most part and spoke fondly of all things German. But they went out of their way to be nice to Audrey's new *Jewish* boyfriend—guilt from the war and all, I assume.

Audrey had just returned from a trip to Italy and was anxious to show me her pictures from the trip, but her mother tried to stop her, and they began having words in another room in both German and English. I couldn't follow the whole conversation, but I was able to ascertain that Audrey's mother objected to showing me the pictures, as they contained images of Audrey's "other boyfriend"—that much I could follow.

My hopes were dashed. However, I faked a smile while leafing through the photo album. As I stated, my dreams and desires for a relationship with Audrey were over. Sad but true.

In thinking about my relationship with Audrey, I also remember that, while we were making out, she would always kiss me with a closed mouth. No exceptions. That fact alone should have given me a hint as to how the relationship was going, but I was too blinded by her beauty to see clearly. I wonder how she kissed her other boyfriends. No, actually, I don't wonder about it.

Conclusion: Audrey was a world traveler and, in retrospect, I think that Audrey probably had a boyfriend in every port—something that I could only aspire to. It would have been hard to land her and still harder to keep her. At the time, the world was her oyster, and I was just a very small part of it. I went away quietly and left her to her other boyfriends. I don't think that I was missed, but, to be honest, she was *definitely* missed.

Eliane: The French Client

One of the cardinal rules of being an attorney is that you should never, ever go to bed with a client.

But, *mon dieu!* Eliane was a pretty French girl with an accent that could melt butter. I was working with her during the day on establishing a business. I was working with her at night on other matters—that is, until one of my law partners strongly suggested that I cease and desist (legal jargon) immediately, which I did.

Eliane understood, and we developed a platonic friendship and continued our attorney-client relationship. It could have gone a lot worse for me, so you may well conclude that I dodged the proverbial Gallic bullet.

Conclusion: I don't know what it is like in your profession, but if you are an attorney, do not mix business with pleasure. It could get you fired. It could get you disbarred. It could only end badly. Save yourself the worry and aggravation. Just say *non* to all Gallic and non-Gallic clients alike.

Jodi and the Bahamian Bodybuilder

Her name was Jodi, and she was one of the most beautiful girls that I had ever seen. Have I said that before? Yes, I'm sure that I have, and I will be saying it at least one more time before this journey ends.

I was at a street festival in Denver with my friend Koni (pronounced "Connie"), a beautiful woman in her own right and a platonic friend of mine for years. I spotted Jodi and couldn't take my eyes off her. I wasn't alone. I was fascinated by the reactions she got from other guys. Men would cross the street to get a better look. Other men were actually barking at her (like dogs—although pigs might be more applicable). As for me, I was too terrified to approach her.

Soon, Jodi and her friends went into a bar. Koni talked me into following them into the bar with the words, "Leave it to me." Okay. We saw her at the bar, and Koni struck up a conversation with her and introduced her to me. Simple. Now it was my turn.

Jodi turned out to be as nice as she was beautiful. She was also intelligent. She was in the mortgage business and also was a part-time bodybuilder. She was not muscle-bound, but she was certainly muscle-perfect. That combined with her perfect face, hair, eyes, legs—a truly magnificent sight to behold!

After conversing for quite some time, we exchanged information—she lived in Calabasas, California—and promised each other that we would keep in touch, and we did. We phoned and corresponded almost daily, and I felt that things were going very well.

I tried to do cute and clever things for her. For instance, she came down with a bad cold, so I sent a "care package" to her via Federal Express with cold medicines, tea, crackers, etc.

Cute, huh? She was thrilled, and I was quite proud of myself. All systems go.

After a couple of months, we decided that I would fly to California to see her. She picked me up at LAX, and I could tell right away that the weekend would not go as well as I had hoped. I was charming, funny, and gregarious—a veritable Noël Coward (a veritable *straight* Noël Coward)—but she just seemed disappointed for some reason.

It turned out that I wasn't the problem at all. She was still carrying a torch for an old boyfriend. That weekend, I heard much more about him than I felt totally necessary. He was a 300-pound full-time bodybuilder from the Bahamas named Victor. Well, if Victor was her type, what could a 145-pound, skinny Jewish attorney do? Nothing, as it turned out.

We spent a pleasant few days together, but as in the Fred Astaire song "A Fine Romance," there were "no clinches" and "no pinches," all because of Victor—at least, I would like to think so.

I returned to Denver. The relationship, if it even could be called that, was over. And I'm sure that Victor got a phone call soon afterward, but not from me.

Conclusion: I think that I handled this one as well as could be expected. But if I had to do it all over again, I would have flown her out to Denver—my turf. It may not have made any difference, but it couldn't have hurt.

Pam: The Temple and the Police

I had been invited to a singles event on a Saturday night at a local temple. Having no other plans, I decided to go—the height of desperation. However, before I went in, registered, and paid my money, I waited at the front door to see the type of women who would be attending. After a half hour, I was about to leave, as no one struck my fancy (which can be painful, I hear).

But wait: a very attractive blonde with great legs arrived—definitely worth checking out. I went in and immediately began to strike up a conversation with her.

Her name was Pam. She was pretty, funny, interesting, and intelligent, and she had great legs. Sorry, I already mentioned that.

The party was a bore for both of us, so we explored all off-limits areas of the temple by ourselves. In the process, we began making out in every dark and empty corner of the temple—shades of my bar mitzvah many years before.

Ultimately, we decided to leave the temple party. We hopped into her car for a drive to a local park to take a walk. Unfortunately (or fortunately, depending on how you look at it), we never left the car. We began making out in the front seat and progressed to making love in the backseat.

Suddenly, I saw a bright light shining on the car from about two blocks away. Of course, it was the police. I have never gotten dressed so fast in my life. We were both in presentable condition by the time the two police officers arrived. They were friendly and understanding, but they had been receiving complaints from people in the neighborhood concerning such practices.

At one point, I asked them whether they were going to arrest me for "breaking and entering." I thought that remark was hilarious. Fortunately, both Pam and the police officers shared my sense of humor, and the officers let us off with a warning to "take it indoors next time."

Pam and I thought that the entire situation was tremendously funny from beginning to end. We saw each other a few more times. She was a great girl, but ultimately we just drifted apart. I regret not having maintained contact with her, but I never will forget her and our encounter with the men in blue.

Conclusion: Okay … okay … I know. Get a room!

Diana: The Giantess

I was having a business lunch with my partner, Curtis, and we both noticed a beautiful girl at the next table—a veritable Barbie doll. We finished eating and left the restaurant. On the way back to the office, all we could talk about was this girl's beauty. Brave soul that I was, I decided to go back to the restaurant and meet her.

I drove back to the restaurant, and she and her two coworkers were still eating. I made up a lame excuse that I had lost my wallet at the table. One thing led to another, and the group invited me to join them. Wow—just like in the movies!

I got to know all three, but Diana, in particular, was very sweet, and we seemed to hit it off quite well. She even gave me her phone number toward the end of the meal. Then her party got ready to leave.

We both stood up to shake hands, and it was then that we both realized she was fully a foot taller than I was. She was as tall as any woman that I had ever met. I felt the blood drain from my body in embarrassment. Thankfully, she didn't say anything, but we were both thinking the same thing.

Alas, it was not meant to be. But at least Curtis was impressed that I had been able to meet her and obtain her telephone number.

Conclusion: I was proud of myself for having the nerve to go back to the restaurant and actually meet her. I never could have guessed at the height difference. I just wish that she had been a little shorter, or that I had been a *lot* taller.

Rachel: Lightning Never Strikes Twice in the Same Place

Recently, I was eating at a Moroccan restaurant and was reminded of a brief encounter that I had with a girl named Rachel.

If you have been paying attention (and I hope that you have), you will have noted that all of my encounters with girls named Rachel have been either very brief or nonexistent. But I keep trying.

In this case, a friend fixed us up. Rachel was a beautiful Eurasian girl with a marvelous butterfly tattoo in the small of her back. And I, of course, was instantly smitten.

On our first date, we went to a Moroccan restaurant where you sit on pillows placed on the floor, are entertained by belly dancers, and eat with your fingers. It was a wonderful evening. We had the restaurant all to ourselves. We fed each other with our fingers in between kisses and ended up making out more than eating. I felt like I was back in high school. It appeared that she felt the same way.

Then it was back to my place. Rachel stayed over that night, but all we did was cuddle. And that was fine with me. I wanted to take it slowly, as I just knew that there was some kind of future with her.

For the next week, I kept calling her to get together. But she always put me off with one excuse or another. Finally, I got her to commit to another date. And, yes, I took her back to the same restaurant, hoping for a repeat of our prior romantic meal.

And ... nothing. Lightning certainly did not strike twice. Rachel was very cool toward me the entire evening. I tried to recapture the magic of our prior date, but it was lost forever. I took her home and never saw her again.

Later, I learned through the grapevine that Rachel had just broken up with her boyfriend prior to our first date. And she had just gotten back together with him prior to our second date. So, basically, I never had a chance.

But I must admit that I still think of Rachel every time that I go to a Moroccan restaurant.

Conclusion: I did the best that I could under the circumstances. I guess that I could have come up with a better plan for our second date. But, as it turned out, it would not have mattered in the least.

Chapter Nine
Foreign Affairs

Spartacus: The Matchmaker

I have always been a great admirer of Kirk Douglas. What other actor could play both Spartacus and Vincent Van Gogh with equal conviction? And I have read with interest each of his first four volumes of memoirs.

As I was reading volume two, *Climbing the Mountain: My Search for Meaning*, a few years ago (a much loftier goal than my search for *women*), I noticed that he mentioned his editor, Ushi, a great deal.

Apparently, Ushi was a good Catholic girl who had converted to Judaism (as was mentioned earlier, Kirk is a devout Jew) and moved to Israel. In the book, there were also some pictures of Ushi, and as I looked at them, I thought that she was the cutest little editor that I ever *did* see. It was then that I decided I would like to get to know her. So what did I do? You already know the answer!

I wrote a nice letter to Kirk, sent him a photo, and asked him if he thought Ushi would like to meet "a nice Jewish attorney." To my surprise, he responded. He told me that he had forwarded my letter and photo to Ushi, that she was a great girl, very Orthodox (a warning?), and that she was living in Jerusalem. He also gave me her e-mail address.

Of course, I wrote to her right away. And we corresponded via e-mail for a month or two. I found Ushi to be very sweet and quite intelligent—just as Kirk had described her in his book.

At one point, she mentioned that Kirk was about to visit her in Jerusalem, and it seemed to me at the time that she was suggesting that I visit her as well. What a grand adventure that trip would have been!

Then she asked me the 64,000-*shekel* question: "How observant of a Jew are you?" Well, I couldn't lie. I told her that I was not very religious. I think that my exact words were "spiritual" and "hopeful agnostic." It was the kiss of death. I didn't hear from her after that.

However, I recently completed reading the fourth volume of Kirk's memoirs. In it, he stated that Ushi had married a rabbi. I e-mailed her again, and she confirmed that she had indeed married a rabbi in the Israeli army, and that she now had two step-*grandchildren*. *Mazel tov!* And belated thanks to Kirk for being so kind.

Conclusion: It never hurts to do semi-outrageous things in the quest for true love. Who knows? It might have worked out, and I could have gotten married in Jerusalem with Spartacus as my best man. Now, that would have been something!

Dr. Cathy: Thailand and the Scottish Doctor

Her name was, and probably still is, Dr. Catherine Watson Brydon—very Scottish, and she had an irresistible Scottish lilt to her voice. We met in Thailand.

Well, ... let's start at the beginning. I was sponsoring an

adorable young Thai girl named Poj-jana near Khon Kaen, Thailand, under one or another foster-parents' plans. I decided that I would like to visit her, so I signed up with a British tour company for a two-week tour of Thailand. The third week I would spend, on my own, traveling to and meeting with my foster child.

During the "get-acquainted" initial meeting of all tour members, I noticed a very sweet-looking girl. She had short dark hair, uneven bangs, a sweet smile, a lovely voice, and great legs. Other than that, she was rather ordinary-looking, but she was the best-looking girl in our tour group—similar in nature to the previously described best-looking girl on the first day of class.

But she was sitting next to and talking with an English guy. What was the situation? Were they together? Just my luck. Or was she available? I found out that she had just met him, so she was available. I began to pay more attention to her, and slowly but surely, I got to know her (actually, not so slowly, but definitely surely). So began an intense mutual flirtation.

On one of the first nights of the tour, we were all supposed to get together and meet in the lobby of the hotel at a certain time. I told her that I would stop by her room to pick her up. She was running late and greeted me wearing nothing but a towel. Okay, I'm easy … I became instantly infatuated.

Each day, we spent more and more time together touring the beautiful country of Thailand. On about day four, I had eaten a rather large Thai meal and had not hydrated sufficiently, and I literally passed out while touring the summer palace north of Bangkok. Later, I was told that I was rushed to a hospital in the Polish ambassador's limo—apparently, he had been touring the summer palace at the same time. What I do remember is that I asked my Scottish doctor, Cathy, to accompany me to the hospital. The rest of the tour members went off without us.

After an IV or two at the hospital, I was feeling refreshed, and Cathy and I returned to "our" hotel room, alone at last.

Cathy had her own room. I, on the other hand, had been rooming with an elderly gentleman from Mauritius. But now I was in Cathy's room to stay—a definite improvement in living arrangements. I recovered quite sufficiently, as we made love all afternoon, before our fellow tour members returned. We joined them for dinner, and neither of us could wipe the smile off our face.

The next week and a half was right out of the best romance novels. I felt like Fabio! We toured the width and breadth of beautiful Thailand, making love all along the way. Looking back on it, I still think that time with Cathy in Thailand contains some of the most romantic moments of my life.

All good things must come to an end, and the two weeks passed all too quickly. Cathy continued on the tour to explore Malaysia, while I took off on my own, heading for Khon Kaen. That first night without her was one of the most miserable experiences of my life. Here I had finally found my soul mate, and now she was gone. Forever? I feared so.

Ultimately, I returned to my law practice in Denver, and she returned to her medical practice in London. What to do? We communicated for nine months or so before we decided that I would fly to London to see her. My plans were to take her to a fancy restaurant and ask her to marry me. The best laid plans … and, boy, did these plans go awry!

I remember getting off the plane at Gatwick Airport and picking up my luggage, all the while expecting to see my dear Cathy run into my arms with tears of joy streaming down her face. I waited and waited … and waited. You guessed it. I flew to London for my big date and got stood up. I was devastated.

I booked a room at a hotel on Oxford Street, called the hospital that Cathy worked at, and was informed that she had high-tailed it back to Galashiels, Scotland, her hometown. I guess that she got cold feet. She was no female Braveheart, that's for sure.

At about 3:00 a.m. that first night, I composed my best

poison-pen letter and mailed it right away, just in case I changed my mind later on. What a great letter—I just wish that I had kept a copy. However, in retrospect, I think that it is fine and dandy to write such letters, but you should never, ever actually mail them.

What was a guy to do? I guess that I could have gone to Scotland to retrieve her just like John Wayne did to Maureen O'Hara in John Ford's classic *The Quiet Man*. (And even though Brydon is a fairly common Scottish name, I think that I could have tracked her down in Galashiels.) Instead, I took advantage of my time in England and spent the next week touring London and taking day trips out of London. I loved it, but it was not exactly the trip that I had expected.

To this day, I've still never been to Scotland. Maybe someday. Maybe not. In fact, the sound of bagpipes still leaves a bad taste in my mouth, not to mention my ears.

I later learned via the Internet that Cathy had moved to Glasgow, Scotland. I wrote to her but never received a response. In fact, I have written to her a number of times over the years. But, alas, nothing but silence.

Sometimes I wonder what her reasons were. How could she do something like that to me? I suppose that it takes all kinds in this world, and to speculate would be a complete waste of time. Although I must admit that I have wasted much too much time in such speculation. In the end, it was a great adventure—both Thailand and London. It could have been worse.

Conclusion: As I have stated before, a holiday romance is never based in reality, no matter how intense or real it seems at the time. Trust me. If you find yourself in a holiday romance, enjoy it for all it's worth, but do not take it too seriously once you arrive home. Holiday memories are great, but home is reality, and the two can never be reconciled. And if you like to travel like me, always keep that in mind.

Afterthought on Thailand: Thailand is a beautiful country, and the people are warm and friendly. Thailand is called "The Land of Smiles," and for good reason.

The Thais take their Buddhist religion very seriously. In fact, it is a crime to take a figure of Buddha out of the country. Of course, that doesn't stop every street vendor from selling them to unsuspecting tourists. In addition, the Thais consider the feet as unclean. For example, it is impolite to point with your feet.

Well, as I was going through customs on my way back from Bangkok to Denver, a customs inspector discovered a Buddha head in my luggage. Alarms went off, and the chief customs inspector arrived—a very stern woman lacking anything that could be called a "smile." I knew that I was really in trouble when it was discovered that I had wrapped the Buddha head in my *socks*! I was taken away for interrogation. After much apologizing and kowtowing, I was free to go, *sans* one Buddha head.

Of course, upon my arrival in Denver, my luggage was nowhere to be found. It took three weeks to finally track it down and retrieve it. I guess that I was being taught a lesson, one that you should remember if you ever venture forth to Thailand.

Jo: Tasmania and the Aussie Dancer

She was one of the most beautiful girls that I have ever seen. I know, I know. Not again, you say. As promised earlier, this is the absolute last time that I will say it.

I had just taken a two-week tour of Australia, where I found the Aussie girls to be beautiful, friendly, and quite approachable. And I had many dates during those first two weeks in Australia.

Now, I was exploring Tasmania on my own for a few days. In case some of you don't know, Tasmania is one of the states in Australia. It is the island just south of the Australian mainland,

and visiting it is like taking a trip back in time to Jane Austen's England: beautiful and quaint. Hobart is the capital and main port city of Tasmania, and for all you trivia buffs, it was the birthplace of Errol Flynn (another hero of mine, for dubious reasons).

I was walking among the shops and restaurants along the pier in Hobart, and suddenly I found myself face-to-face with "a perfect ten." She had a perfect face, a perfect smile, and a perfect dancer's body. I knew that I *had* to get to know her.

Before I proceed, please note that I have not used a numbering system to describe any of the other women detailed in this book. First, I find it demeaning and sexist. (Yes, even I think so.) Second, I find the terms not very useful. I have noticed, however, that "perfect tens" tend to be friendlier, more sincere, and more approachable than sevens, eights, or nines. Those latter women sometimes have a chip on their shoulder, as they are not tens, and they tend to be more self-absorbed and less friendly to men. That's just my observation.

Back to our story … where were we? Oh yes, I just *had* to get to know her. Being a brave soul, I went up to her and started talking to her. She was delightful and very friendly. Her name was Jo, and she was a dancer with the Sydney Dance Company. They were just completing a tour of Australia, and that night was their final performance in the small theatre (as the Aussies spell it) in Hobart. One thing led to another, and we arranged to meet after the performance for a drink. Perfect.

Yes, perfect, except … oh, no … I had just completed almost three weeks of touring Australia, and I didn't have an appropriate outfit to wear to the theatre. No problem. I had all afternoon to shop in Hobart for a decent outfit. Big problem. Hobart is a lovely city, but there were no quality men's clothing stores in the entire city. At least, I didn't find any. I did the best that I could—nice shirt, black vest, new denim jeans. (I know, I know, but it was the best that I could do.)

I put my new outfit on, bought a dozen long-stemmed red

roses, and made my way to the theatre, feeling very much like William Holden. I asked one of the attendants to deliver the flowers backstage to "my friend Jo." He asked, "What's her last name?" I confessed that I did not know. He responded, "She must be a close friend." Everyone is a comedian ... but the flowers were delivered.

After the performance, which was a series of modern/jazz dances in which she was good, but not great, I went backstage and searched for her. Time went by, the theatre emptied, and I still couldn't find her. Oh, no (again!) Finally, I saw her in the dressing room, all alone. She had been waiting for me and thought that I had stood her up. Not a chance.

We had a wonderful after-performance snack of champagne and dessert, accompanied by a delightful conversation. Sadly, my dream date ended all too quickly. We exchanged information and corresponded, fitfully, for about six months or so.

Later, she advised me that she had accepted a job dancing in Amsterdam and that she would contact me from there. I was curious as to what type of dancing she would be doing in Amsterdam. But I never got the chance to find out, as I never heard from her again. So, Jo, if you ever read this tome, I would love to hear from you.

Conclusion: Was this really a holiday romance or just a fun first-meeting story? Probably a bit of both. Still, the fates and the probabilities were against it. But sometimes you just have to go for it, regardless of the ultimate outcome. No regrets. Okay, maybe just one regret—that I did not move to Amsterdam.

Vanda: San Diego and the Russian Model

I have met women in many different ways, but this one was an exceptional meeting, even for me.

I had signed up with an international pen-pal service

whereby you could correspond with women from all over the world. (Desperation? You bet!) This particular service featured women primarily from countries of the former Soviet Union and from Asia.

I had dated Russian and Asian women before and had enjoyed dating many, but not all, of them. There is something intriguing about foreign women, at least for me.

Through this service I met Vanda, a fashion model living in Moscow. I saw her photo in the "girl catalog," wrote her a nice letter enclosing a photo of myself, and received a sweet letter and some beautiful photos in return. The Internet was in its infancy at the time, so we corresponded mostly by regular mail and fax.

Vanda seemed like a very sweet girl, and those photos … be still my heart! She was incredibly sexy and gorgeous. Where was this going to lead? I was not about to fly to Moscow to meet her. (You will recall my experience in London with, I mean *without*, Dr. Cathy.) Then Vanda mentioned that she would be in San Diego for a photo shoot and asked if I would meet her there. Would I? You bet! And just in case, … I had never been to San Diego, so I would enjoy exploring there by myself if it came to that.

I booked myself a room at a downtown hotel, rented a car, and waited for her call. Thankfully, the call came. We arranged to have dinner that night. I picked her up where she was staying, and we had a lovely dinner. And, yes, it was the same person that I had been corresponding with. And, yes, she most definitely had to be a fashion model. She was *amazing*!

We spent a few days together, but like many Russian women that I have known, she had a very dour personality. Picture Natasha Fatale of Boris and Natasha fame.

What I couldn't get over was her lack of enthusiasm for her surroundings. I was so impressed: the Pacific Ocean, the Gaslamp Quarter, Coronado Island, etc. I kept asking her if she liked this or that aspect of San Diego, and it was always, "*Nyet!*

Nyet!" She was from dank Moscow and was not at all impressed with gorgeous San Diego. What was wrong with her?

I eventually found out what was wrong. One night I was driving her back from a lovely dinner at Croce's (shameless plug), and we saw a limousine that was literally two blocks long—the longest limo that I had ever seen. Vanda looked at me and said, "That is first thing I see in United States I am impressed" (her exact words—accent and all).

From that point on, I knew that this relationship had no hope. How do you spell "shallow" in Russian? V-A-N-D-A. She was ten times more shallow than I was.

Our time was up, and we parted amiably, never to see each other again. I would occasionally see her on various international pen-pal websites, but I never did communicate with her again. In the end, I hope that she found all the stretch limos that her heart desired.

Conclusion: You pays your money (or *rubles*), and you takes your chances. And I truly did enjoy beautiful San Diego, despite Vanda. If you are ever in a similar situation, just relax and enjoy your surroundings, even if that enjoyment is not shared by your companion. And if she is a model from Moscow, you can bet that enjoyment will *not* be shared.

Montreal and the Nameless Indonesian Girl

The same international pen-pal service and, basically, the same result.

This correspondent was a pretty girl from Indonesia, and even though we corresponded for some months, her name escapes me.

In any event, she was planning a trip to visit relatives in Montreal and asked if I would join her for a few days. I had never been to Montreal, so ... here I go again!

Montreal was not a disappointment in the least. Unfortunately, I can't say the same thing about the rest of the trip.

We had planned to meet at one of the shopping centers in downtown Montreal, and we did. But from the moment we met, we both knew that there was absolutely no chemistry between us. We tried to have a pleasant time for a few days, but I'm sure that we were both counting the hours until I had to leave Montreal and return to work. Obviously, we did not stay in touch, but I loved Montreal.

However, falling in love with a city is never quite as satisfying as falling in love with a girl. As you can tell by now, I've had ample experience at both.

Conclusion: There must be mutual chemistry for a relationship to flourish. If there is no spark, there will be no flame, and a flame is a "good thing," as Martha Stewart might say.

Alexandra Hartman: The Aussie Girl Who Did Not Exist

Again, the same international dating site, but with a much different result.

She said that her name was Alexandra Hartman and she was from Perth, Australia. She had drop-dead gorgeous pictures. She also told me that she was a medical student. She said that her father, Dr. Alex Hartman, was a noted surgeon who had recently died.

And Alexandra seemed to like me a lot. In fact, from the very start, she seemed to like me almost too much to be believed—a clear warning sign. More on that in a second.

By the way, have you ever had international phone sex? Believe me, it can get expensive, but it can also be a lot of fun. I must give her credit. Besides that, she was also a gifted conversationalist. She was incredibly knowledgeable about many topics, like art, history, politics, movies, and so on. At least, she talked a good game.

As with anything in life, if it sounds too good to be true, it is. Eventually I got suspicious, as Alexandra just sounded too good to be true. She would always tell me that she was falling in love with me. But when I would suggest that we meet, she was always vague about making plans to get together. Finally, she just seemed to have entirely too much time on her hands to be a medical student.

So I decided to engage a private detective in Perth, which was far easier and less expensive than you might guess.

I discovered that there had never been a Dr. Alex Hartman, dead or alive, and that there was no Alexandra Hartman registered in any of the local medical schools. In fact, there was no Alexandra Hartman, *period*. However, she had given me her address—a home, I found out, that was owned and occupied by a Mr. Victor and Ms. Yvonne Keenan.

Armed with this knowledge, I was able to catch her in many lies. I never confronted her with the truth, as it really didn't matter by then. And I stopped communicating with her very shortly thereafter.

Apparently, Yvonne was (and probably still is) a bored and lonely housewife in Perth who gets her jollies by impersonating a beautiful Aussie girl for all the attention that it brings her. Sad, really, but I guess that everyone must have a hobby.

Conclusion: As I previously stated … and this goes for anything in life, including women: if it sounds too good to be true, it is. Just walk away, and forget about it.

Chapter Ten
Match.com and Other Disasters

My dad and I once speculated on the number of women that I have gone out with since first attending college at the age of eighteen. We concluded that the number was close to a thousand.

That number may seem inflated to you, but consider the fact that I have never been married, I have dated a lot of women, I am in my fifties, and this number includes not only past relationships, but also those women whom I might have met for coffee for a half hour and would never see again. There have been quite a few of the latter type of dates.

Any comparisons to Wilt Chamberlain would be completely erroneous on your part.

Speaking of numbers, I am fascinated by people's obsession with "The Number." By that, I mean the number of people that one has slept with. I used to think that it was a guy thing, but many women are interested in The Number as well. As for me, my number is not nearly as high as you would think, but more than it should be. Yes, I think that you can sleep with too many people. You get a bit jaded, and that is never a good thing.

As for my one-date affairs (a bad choice of words), some have been more humorous and/or interesting than my multi-date affairs. Well, let's just say more humorous than interesting.

As I state in the next chapter, Match.com is not a bad way to meet women, but I think that you will find that most "Match dates" will be one-date adventures (or disasters). But that rule applies to most dates, no matter how you meet them.

The following is just a sampling of some of those dating disasters, both Match and non-Match. Many of them were one-date disasters, but I have also included a few multi-date girls whose stories ended just as disastrously. Perhaps "disaster" is too strong a term. You will find neither the Hindenburg crash nor the Battle of Stalingrad described here, but, in Barry World, these stories would be considered disasters.

Rachel the Stripper

I was walking to the swimming pool in my old townhome complex when suddenly I saw a vision of loveliness sitting on a balcony and talking on the phone.

She was a beautiful brunette with a lovely figure and gorgeous tanned legs. As she was on the phone, I slipped her my business card, having written on the back, "Call me—I have a million questions to ask you." She called the next day. Yes! This could be the start of something big (an old song by Steve Allen, I believe).

The next week we had dinner, and she was delightful. She was not only beautiful, but quite intelligent as well. And I began to like her a lot.

Her name was Rachel, and she was an exotic dancer at one of the higher-end "gentlemen's clubs" in town. I was proud to say that I had never been there (and still haven't), but I didn't hold it against her. She said that she was going to "perform" for two years and save all her money for college. I was impressed. (By the way, I do not look down on women who make their living in this way. However, I do think that the guys who frequent these places and throw their money away are complete idiots.)

After dinner, I asked her back to my place. She declined and said that she would rather sit on *her* balcony and talk. We did so for a few minutes until we were interrupted by a tall, muscular fellow without a neck who demanded to know who I was. I asked him the same question—I was braver back then. As it turned out, he was her long-standing boyfriend, and Rachel knew he would be arriving around that time. I had been cruelly used.

She had used her date with an attorney to make her Neanderthal boyfriend jealous, and it worked. I left before things got out of hand with life and limb (mine) intact. It was disappointing, but not totally unexpected. I never saw hide nor hair of her again.

And another potential relationship with a girl named Rachel bites the dust!

Lisa, a.k.a. Hulk Hogan

It started out well. We met at an art gallery, and, apparently, she enjoyed the fine arts just as much as I did.

Her name was Lisa. She was from Alabama and had the cutest Southern accent. As I picked her up for our first date, she presented me with a flower. How sweet! Nothing could go wrong with this one, right? Wrong.

I made the mistake of sleeping with her that first night, and, to put it mildly, she liked things rough. I, on the other hand, like things a bit more gentle—just a personal preference. To each his or her own. (Or as we used to say in Texas, "that's why there is chocolate and vanilla.") However, when we were done, I distinctly remember going into the bathroom to check my body for scratches and bruises. I felt like I had just gone ten rounds with Mike Tyson.

After that encounter, I reluctantly made the unilateral

decision that the relationship was over. And I never saw her again, as she moved back to Alabama shortly thereafter.

Cynthia the Fashion Disaster

Cynthia was wonderful in so many ways: a blue-eyed blonde with a lovely figure and a sweet disposition.

But—and I couldn't get over it—she was a complete fashion disaster. Her fashion sense was nonexistent, and it drove me crazy.

Now, I am no Beau Brummell, but I do have a modicum of fashion sense, and I really appreciate a girl who knows how to dress well. I guess that the attempted relationship with Cynthia was a nonstarter to begin with. Perhaps I just should have taken her shopping. Perhaps daily.

About a year after I stopped seeing her, my girlfriend *du jour* and I ran into her at the mall. There had been no improvement in her appearance. I think that any attempted styling on my part would have been fruitless.

Shallow on my part, I admit, but … such a waste.

Sunny, Kim, and the Korean Switch

I met two beautiful Korean roommates who both worked at a sushi restaurant that I used to frequent. I liked them both right away.

Sunny was tall and thin with beautiful long black hair and a thick Korean accent. She was so beautiful that just watching her wait on her customers was almost a religious experience!

Kim was shorter with a pretty face, short black hair, and no trace of a Korean accent—much more Americanized.

For some reason, I asked out Sunny first, and we had a few dates. But it wasn't clicking into place for me. So I decided that I would prefer to date Kim.

The problem was how to effect "the switch"—stop dating one roommate and start dating the other. Well, I called Kim and arranged for a date, and we did meet for dinner. However, throughout dinner, she just kept emphasizing to me what a great girl she thought Sunny was.

Unfortunately, Kim was more interested in getting me back together with Sunny than getting involved with me herself. We parted friends, but I never called Sunny back. And it obviously went nowhere with Kim.

For once in my life, I had attempted the switch and failed miserably. Oh, well. Nothing ventured, nothing gained.

Kristi the Swing Dancer

Kristi was a Match.com disaster, as are most of the date descriptions that follow.

Kristi was an attractive brunette with a great sense of humor. We met for lunch and had a nice time, so we decided to take swing dance lessons together. Later in the week, we met at the dance hall, and I paid for a month of lessons for both of us, consisting of one lesson a week. I was terrible, but I thought that we had a nice time.

As you can guess, I showed up the next week, and Kristi was nowhere to be seen—no phone call, no e-mail, nothing. Well, at least I enjoyed the last three lessons. I didn't improve much, but it was fun. And I learned everything about Kristi that I needed to know.

Lydia the Aussie "Hottie"

One of my pet peeves is a girl referring to herself as "hot" or a "hottie."

Lydia did both. We were on our first (and only) date, and, to be fair, she was a nice girl and did bear a passing resemblance to Jennifer Aniston—just a passing resemblance, mind you. But she kept referring to herself as "hot."

Not only was it a turnoff, but I didn't have the heart to tell her that she wasn't all that hot. We never saw each other again. I am sure that some other guy thought that she was indeed hot. Good luck to both of them.

Ashley and the Doggy Bag

Another pet peeve of mine is a dinner date who orders way too much food and packs it all into doggy bags to feast on for the next few days.

Ashley was even worse. She ordered an expensive dessert to go. She did not even order it for herself, but explained to me that she was bringing it back to her roommate's sons, who she thought would really enjoy it.

I bit my tongue, but inside I was seething. How rude! I couldn't wait to get away from her. I hope that those sweet young boys got tummy-aches. Sorry, bad attitude.

Olga and Her Cell Phone

There seem to be a lot of Russian and Ukrainian immigrants on Match.com. I believe that I know the reason why—free meals and/or the possibility of a green card.

Anyway, Olga was a true Russian beauty. We met at a restaurant for dinner, and I could tell right away that I was not her cup of *borscht*. When that happens to me, I still try to make the evening as pleasant as possible.

Olga, on the other hand, spent most of the evening in the restroom—no doubt furiously calling friends on her cell phone and trying to arrange alternative plans.

People have since told me that I should have paid the bill and left her. I guess that I was just too much of a gentleman.

I waited for her, and, thankfully, the evening did not last too long.

Jane: The Mouth that Roared

Mercifully, I do not remember her name, so I will just refer to her as "Jane Doe." And that is being kind!

I knew that I was in trouble during our first phone conversation when I could not get a single word in edgewise—not one word. Finally, I called my home phone from my cell phone, and I informed her that I had a call from my mom and had to get off the phone.

My mistake was in agreeing to meet her for dinner. Jane was late and apologized by planting a wet, sloppy kiss on my lips. As you already know by now, I am no prude. But that is one kiss I could have done without. Get to know me for at least a few minutes before you kiss me, please!

If I thought that the face-to-face meeting would go better than the telephone conversation, I was sadly mistaken. I still could not get a word in edgewise.

I ate as fast as I could and shot pleading glances at our waitress in the hope that she would hurry up with the check. I got out of there as quickly as humanly possible and with at least most of my sanity intact. Dreadful.

Svetlana and the Kisses

Another Russian girl ... well, actually in Svetlana's case, a Ukrainian girl. There's not much difference, really.

For your future reference, Russian/Ukrainian girls will always ask to meet at expensive restaurants for dinner. And it is usually the dinners that they are after, not you. No quick coffee dates for these girls! In any event, Svetlana was cute and seemed rather sweet.

Dinner was enjoyable—expensive, but enjoyable. The restaurant was in a nice shoppette, so we went window shopping, started to hold hands, and, yes, even kiss. In fact, there was a lot of kissing going on. I thought that this one might actually turn into something. Wrong.

Later, I called and e-mailed, but I never received a response from her and never saw her again. What happened? Well, it was probably the case that she had another date shortly thereafter (maybe even that same day) and that she preferred him to me. Fickle? Yes. Shallow? You bet.

I just chalked it up to another bad experience with a daughter of Russia or Ukraine. Maybe I should change my mind and always buy American. Maybe.

Kate the Opera Singer

Kate appeared pretty near perfect. Her pictures were beautiful, her profile was fascinating, and she was an opera singer.

What a great match for me: someone who also was very interested in the arts, and someone with the talent to actually make a living at it.

We carried on an e-mail correspondence for a couple of weeks, and I started to become very interested in her. We even began sending flirtatious e-mails. So what happened?

Well, we met! And God bless her, but her pictures had to be at least ten years old. And she outweighed me by at least twenty pounds. I felt misled and just a bit used. Apparently, she was not too crazy about me, either.

But it was only a quick coffee date, so we both were very cordial knowing that our date would soon be over.

The World's Shortest Date

This date lasted not more than ten minutes. I swear! Confused? So was I. In fact, I still am.

We initially chatted over the phone and seemed to get along just fine. So we arranged to meet at a nearby restaurant for dinner. During our first few minutes at the restaurant, she peppered me with questions about my book, my law career, and my life in general. I answered her questions in detail. Maybe too much detail?

After ten minutes or so, she suddenly got up and said, "I can't do this," and she started to leave the restaurant. Frankly, I didn't care either way, but I asked her what the problem was. She told me that I had not stopped talking about myself since we met. I apologized but silently was pleased about her departure. As I stated, not more than ten minutes had elapsed.

This experience was unique for me. I thought that she was asking me questions because she was interested in hearing the answers and getting to know me. I had planned to learn about her by then asking her questions of my own. A little give and take. But it was not meant to be.

In retrospect, I am sure that her departure had very little to do with me or our date. There definitely was something else going on. But, luckily for me, she wasted only ten minutes of my life. I have a feeling that sitting through a whole dinner with her would have been more of a burden than I would have cared to bear.

Holly, Sexting, and Faking It

Holly was a pretty blonde. And she was from Colorado, so we had something in common. But, in looking back on it, I think that was about all that we had in common.

We began e-mailing each other daily. And sooner rather than later, our e-mailing turned into sexting. She actually was pretty good at it. And I consider myself a fairly good writer. So I think that I gave as good as I got. (Well, at least I kept up!)

One thing led to another, and she invited me over for the evening. I brought some Chinese food, and we shared a nice meal.

After dinner, she immediately asked me to braid her hair in pigtails (or "handles" as my friend Ashleigh calls them). And, yes, we ended up in bed.

It was terrible! I was terrible. She was terrible. The entire experience was terrible. And, yes, I even faked an orgasm in the hope that the evening would be a short one. I am not at all sure that I fooled her, but I didn't hang around long enough to find out.

It was a very short date, and when it was over, we never communicated with each other again. And that was just fine with me. And with her too, I suspect.

Frankly, I think that I am just too old for one-night stands. That *is* possible, isn't it? I'd like to think so.

Lasagna the Ukrainian Nurse

I would like to submit one last "Match girl" for your consideration.

Her name was not actually Lasagna. It was Svitlana. But, over time, my family and friends began calling her Lasagna for some strange reason, and the name stuck.

Lasagna was a pretty dark-haired nurse originally from Ukraine. (I know, I know. Not again!) I liked her right away and enjoyed spending time with her. We even took ballroom dance classes together. And she showed up for all of the classes, thank God. However, I always got mixed signals from her. Very mixed, indeed.

On the one hand, she would always tell me that she hoped that I was seeing other people. On the other hand, she seemed to love to hug and kiss me. She was always so affectionate every single time that we got together.

It confused me until my friend Koni told me that, in all probability, Lasagna's "love language" was physical affection. That was just what she enjoyed and how she communicated. It had very little to do with me. Lasagna had many male friends, and I am sure that she acted the same way with them as well.

The whole thing was all rather disappointing and distasteful. So my feelings for Lasagna ran the gamut from like to infatuation to disdain to complete indifference. I wish her well, but I am glad that she is out of my life.

Zyla the Homeless Lesbian

I met Zyla at a bookstore, and we seemed to hit it off right away. She was cute but way too young. How young? I am not sure, but still *way too young*.

By the way, her given name was Misty, but she had recently changed it to Zyla. Go figure.

Zyla wasn't working or going to school. She was just living off the kindness of strangers (shades of a modern-day Blanche DuBois) for food and shelter.

We went out twice, and although things never clicked into place, I did enjoy her company. We even kissed a bit.

Then my friends at the bookstore told me that they were all quite sure that she was a lesbian. It had never even occurred to me. But, you know, I think that their instincts were right on the mark. How could I have missed it?

Well, it really didn't matter, as I never saw her again. I just hope that she found a home … and a girlfriend.

Chapter Eleven
Dating Services That I Have Known

Great Expectations

Great Expectations is a video-dating service. I tend to view this service as one of low expectations.

They have very attractive and slick saleswomen, and they talk a good game. They even show you pictures of very beautiful "available" women in their system. As it turns out, many of these women are "on freeze," meaning that they are not available.

My experience has been that I have rejected most of the women that have chosen me and vice versa. Could that old Groucho line come into play here? "I would never join any club that would have me as a member."

To be fair, I have had two very good female friends who have met their husbands through Great Expectations. So there you have it.

It's Just Lunch

This service interviews you and then fixes you up with other members, sight unseen, for lunch.

Again, they have an attractive and slick sales staff who practically gush that they have so many of the type of women that you are seeking.

However, after a few lunch dates, I became convinced that they don't really listen or try to match you appropriately. They just try to match you as quickly as possible so that, hopefully, you will re-sign with them.

I had a number of conversations with my representative, but all to no avail. I finally gave up before my membership was over.

Eight-Minute Dating

There are a number of "speed-dating" services, but I think that this one is the best known. It's not bad, really.

You meet eight different people over eight minutes, and then, the next day, you log onto their site and choose the ones that interest you. If they also choose you, you get their names and phone numbers.

It's a cute idea, and I've been to about a half dozen of their events. However, I have not had too much success with this service. Don't ask me why. Perhaps I shall try it again.

eHarmony

You all have heard their ads on radio and TV, and it sounds great. You fill out an online form, which takes about forty-five minutes, you submit it and pay a fee, and then they fix you up with your "soul mate."

Unfortunately, I did not get past their online survey. After

I concluded it, I was advised that they could not help me. Do you think that they can diagnose "shallow" online?

I actually know many people who have been rejected, both male and female. The only similarities that I can see are that we all responded that we were "spiritual" or not religious. And I think that this service is a faith-based (Christian) service. At least that is my impression.

The men and women that I have talked to who were not rejected have all told me that they were not at all impressed with their matching process. But, … I never got the chance to find out for myself.

Match

So far, this service has been the best one for me. You post your photos and profile online and connect with others who have done the same.

This site is most like the real dating world, and you get the good, the bad, and the ugly. Some photos are old, and some profiles are dishonest. But, for the most part, it is a pretty good and inexpensive way to jump into the world of online dating.

Hopefully, the following is a helpful hint: once you have met someone online, do not spend an inordinate amount of time exchanging e-mails or engaging in telephone conversations. You may be wasting a whole lot of time and getting yourself worked up for nothing. Meeting is key.

So, once you've connected online, arrange to meet right away. Then, if it doesn't work out, you haven't wasted a lot of time or mental energy.

Meetup

In many cities, such as Denver and San Diego, there is a city-specific website called Meetup. Here you can search for groups with specific interests and meet others with those same interests.

Whether you like to bike or hike or wish to learn French cooking or ballroom dancing, there probably will be a group for you to join to meet like-minded individuals and maybe even like-minded women.

Cherry Blossoms

This one is an international online dating service featuring mostly women from Asian countries and countries of the former Soviet Union. It is inexpensive—a one-time fee per year—and there are thousands of women to choose from.

I guess that the idea is that you connect by e-mail, arrange to visit her, and then, if you get along, fly her to the United States on a fiancée visa. I have never taken it nearly that far, but I have corresponded with many women and have even met a couple of them whom you have already read about.

However, beware: there are numerous scammers (those who are looking for money) and spammers (those who steer you to other paying sites, such as translation services). Just be careful and be smart. If a girl falls in love with you after the first few e-mails, run away fast.

Anastasia

Anastasia is one of *many* international online dating sites focusing on Russian and Ukrainian women, and it has literally thousands of pictures of beautiful women. (I wish that I owned a Glamour Shots franchise in Moscow!) It is an expensive site, as you are charged for each e-mail sent and received, and that can add up to big bucks.

In addition, I question whether all of the women on this site are genuine. For example, I was writing to one woman for a while and then quit the site. A few months later, I rejoined, and she was still on the site. So I wrote to her again, and when she answered, it was just as if I had never corresponded with her. She didn't seem to know who I was. Either she had a very bad memory (unlikely), or her picture was being used by the company to elicit a steady stream of e-mails. (Or, horror of horrors, her picture was being used by a fat naked man in his basement in Moscow!) You decide.

To be fair, Anastasia has one of the better reputations for this type of business, so they must be doing something right. Again, just try to be careful and be smart. They are in business to make money, after all.

Chapter Twelve
Some Conclusions on Life, Liberty, and the Pursuit of Women

What have I learned after all of this? Precious little, I suspect. But, in addition to the conclusion at the end of each story above, there are certain other rules (a few repeated for emphasis) that I now try to live by—as follows:

1. Always pick Mary Ann.
2. Always pick Tonya.
3. Always pick Betty.
4. As stated by Antoine de Saint-Exupéry in his novel *The Little Prince*, follow the dictum "It is only with the heart that one can see rightly. The essential is invisible to the eye."
5. As stated by *me*, beauty is only skin deep. The older you get, the more you will realize the truth of this particular pearl of wisdom.
6. Knowledge gained through experience is costly wisdom. I don't know who first told me that, but think about it. I think that it actually has some relevance to the topics at hand.

7. Always take the high road. Always do the honorable thing. You will be surprised at the number of times that this action will not be reciprocated. But do so anyway, as it is the right thing to do.

8. Do unto others as you would have them do unto you. Always follow "The Golden Rule." It is called The Golden Rule for a reason, and it has been around since at least the time of Confucius. Again, even if your action is not reciprocated, treat her as you would wish to be treated.

9. The grass is never greener. Quit looking over the fence at your neighbor's lawn (or wife). His grass is not greener, no matter what it may look like to you. Cultivate and appreciate the relationship that you have instead of wishing it was something or someone else. The more active that you are in looking for greener pastures, the less successful you will be in maintaining a stable and healthy relationship.

10. Don't be like the proverbial kid in the candy store. Don't feel like you have to taste every different kind of candy in the store. If you are enjoying one piece, stick with it. Avoid the tummy-ache. I hope that this analogy makes sense to you—it's a pretty easy one to decipher.

11. Never, ever take anyone for granted. If you are in a stable and committed relationship, thank your lucky stars. Think every day about what you can do to make her happy—anything from giving her a small gift to taking out the garbage. Make it a conscious effort every single day. I know that it is extremely difficult, if not almost impossible. The alternative is the possibility of losing a relationship, which you may regret for the rest of your life.

12. First impressions are pretty reliable. I would stick with them.

13. Before approaching any girl, always check the ring finger. If there is a ring there, of any kind, walk away. She is either engaged/married, or she may be wearing it for protection to ward off guys like me. In any event, it is not worth pursuing.

14. Girls generally are not interested in "trading up" (or, in fairness, "trading down"). If you meet a girl, and she is from a vastly different (especially lower) socioeconomic background than you are, odds are that she will not be interested in you. I have encountered this situation a number of times. Women prefer to date men within their own social "milieu." (I love that word!) That's just the way it is. Don't try to change it. Just accept it as a fact and move on.

15. Girls do not like liars. Do not tell lies—even little white lies. I used to fudge my age by just a couple of years on my Match.com profile. It was the kiss of death. Even if a girl was interested in me, it was all over after I confessed my real age. I had committed an unpardonable sin. So be truthful in all things, and let the chips fall where they may.

16. Follow the "three-date rule." If a romance has not developed by the end of the third date, the odds are that it never will. So either accept it and keep her around as a friend, or continue your search, or both.

17. Do not become a "stage door Johnny." In the olden days, these were men who waited at the stage door of a theater for an actress to appear after a show. In a more modern sense, these are men who are romantically interested in a certain woman, can never get past the friendship stage, and wait around hoping for romance. It never, ever happens. All good things do *not* come to those who wait. So, again, once

you are slotted in the "friend" category, either accept it or move on.

18. Never, ever (ever!) date a woman who is married, or even just separated. This conclusion should be a no-brainer, but you would be surprised at how often it is ignored. I have even ignored it once or twice myself. If the relationship was meant to be, it will survive the time that it takes to have a divorce granted. (Listen to your attorney!) And if it doesn't survive, it wasn't a worthwhile relationship to begin with.

19. Conversely, don't *you* ever date anyone while *you* are married or in an exclusive relationship. It is a rule that many men violate at one time or another. Again, I am guilty of it myself. But it can only lead to disaster and heartbreak on any number of different levels.

20. Long-distance relationships never last. I don't care if you are in a different city, state, or country; ultimately, you will be disappointed. The only exception that I have encountered is in so-called "open relationships," wherein two people lead separate lives, especially sexually. I hear that Shirley MacLaine was married for decades to a husband who resided permanently in Japan. But if you actually want to spend time with your significant other, stay within the same geographic area.

21. There is nothing worse than a lost opportunity. If you see someone you are interested in, go for it. Approach her. The worst thing that can happen is that you will be rejected. Big deal. There is a scene in the movie *Citizen Kane* where the Everett Sloane character, as an old man, is describing a beautiful woman that he once saw in his youth. Even many years later, he could describe her exactly and was still upset with himself for not attempting to get to know

her. I have had many such lost opportunities myself, and I remember quite a few of them. Make the effort. Sure, you may get rejected and feel foolish, but that scenario is better than not making the effort at all.

22. A caveat to rule twenty-one above—don't try to hit on attractive bartenders or flight attendants. These women are bothered by men like me every minute of their working lives. Give them a break. And give yourself a break, as you will in all probability be unsuccessful. Don't even consider these women as opportunities that you will regret losing—they are not.

23. Once you've decided to abide by these rules or rules of your own, do not break any of them at any time or for any girl. You will be tempted. I know. I know. "This girl is different. I will make an exception in her case." Big mistake. Don't do it.

24. Always bear in mind Albert Einstein's definition of insanity: doing the same thing over and over again and expecting different results. I'm just guessing, but I'll bet that Einstein fellow was probably one smart cookie.

25. Finally, on a lighter note, we have something in our family called "love presents." These are small gifts that we give for no special reason other than to say, "I am thinking of you." Give some love presents. I bet that it will make you feel as good as the recipient does—it always does for me!

Postscript

As I was writing this book, my dad, Charles Rothman, died. He passed away six days after my parents' fifty-eighth wedding anniversary.

Although this book deals with romantic relationships, let me say a word about family relationships. Enjoy your relationships with family members while you can, as you never know how long you will be lucky enough to have these people in your life. Don't let petty things get in the way. And don't ever forget to keep saying "I love you." It will do your heart good.

One more thing … my mom always used to tell me that God goes in alphabetical order. If so, I am not sure whether He/She goes by first name or last name. Once I figure it out, I'll let you know.